DOING HISTORY

J. H. HEXTER

DOING HISTORY

Indiana University Press

Bloomington & London

Published in Canada by Fitzhenry & Whiteside Limited, Don Mills, Ontario

Library of Congress catalog card number: 70-165049

ISBN: 0-253-31820-3

Manufactured in the United States of America

CONTENTS

To my children
Christopher
Eleanor
Anne
Richard

PREFACE

"THE Rhetoric of History" first appeared in the *International Encyclopedia* of the *Social Sciences* under the heading HISTORIOGRAPHY: "The Rhetoric of History." "History and the Social Sciences" was offered as a report to the 13th International Congress of Historical Sciences held in Moscow in August, 1970. Some of the observations in the report reflect the specific geographic and political milieu in which it was presented. Nevertheless, it did not seem desirable to me to strike out the particular comments evoked by that milieu. It seemed preferable simply to advise the reader in advance of the relation between some of the observations in the paper and the circumstances under which it was delivered.

The article entitled "Doing History" was published in the *Journal of Contemporary History*, Volume II, 1967, pp. 5–23 under the title "Some American Observations." The essay entitled "The Historian and His Society: A Sociological Analysis—Perhaps" was published in *Commentary*, June, 1971, under the title "Doing History." "Garrett Mattingly, Historian" was published in *From the Renaissance to the Counter-Reformation*, a volume of essays published by Random House in honor of that historian among my contemporaries whom I most admire. The sources in which they originally appeared have kindly granted me permission to reprint the articles included in this volume.

The alteration made in titles may seem to indicate an unseemly interest in merely cosmetic aspects of the contents of this book. One would prefer to think that a rose by any other name would smell as sweet; on the other hand, recollecting Camembert cheese, one is not quite certain. In any case, "Doing History" was suggested to me as a title by Mr. Murdoch Matthew of the Indiana University Press last year. My frequent uses of it since indicate how felicitous I found it to be. For everything else in the book I am solely responsible.

As to the dedicatees of *Doing History*, my children, in order of age, Christopher, Eleanor, Anne and Richard, needless to say, they had nothing at all to do with the book. Nevertheless, they are dear children, and it is about time I dedicate a book to them.

DOING HISTORY

1/

By Way of Introduction

THE genesis of each of the essays in *Doing History* was literally casual, all the pieces having been written not in conformity to and as part of a predetermined plan, but as the result of particular accidents generated from without—invitations to deliver a lecture and a report, requests from a journal for an article and from an encyclopedia for a contribution. If the invitations had not come, it is quite possible that the particular pieces in this book would not have been written.

These somewhat chaotic origins of the contents of this book, did, however, have a certain advantage. Being solicited to express my views, rather than being a solicitor for an opportunity to express them, I could afford to insist on writing my own ticket. The Soviet hosts to the International Congress of the Historical Sciences were inhibited from blue pencilling any *ne kulturnyi* remarks in "History and the Social Sciences" by rules which deprive the country that acts as innkeeper to the Congress from censoring the critical comments of the guests. Had the editors of the *Journal of Contemporary History* wanted to modify or to eliminate from their review the piece, "Doing History," they would have been frustrated by circumstances. As a result of a lapse of memory on my part, the manuscript arrived in their editorial office only two days before the journal was scheduled to go to press.

The liberty of the piece "The Rhetoric of History" came by way of an explicit pact negotiated in advance with the editors of the *International Encyclopedia of the Social Sciences*, and honored by them graciously and beyond the call of duty. My previous dealings with the *Encyclopedia* had been confined to a brief exchange of letters, waspish on my part. In about 1962 a letter from the editor requested me to do an article for the *Encyclopedia* on Thomas More (1478–1535) for, as I recall, $35.00. Enclosed with the letter was a seventeen-part editorial directive indicating among other things that the biography should deal with More's relations to the social sciences and with the relevance of his work to underdeveloped nations. My reply thanked the editor for his munificent offer. It pointed out, however, that the *Encyclopedia* had not seen fit to include a historian on its editorial board, and that my fellow historians might think ill of me if I took the place that the board assigned to our discipline "at the sink and amid the slops of the social sciences." On the matter of a biography of Thomas More, I heard nothing further from the editor. I did get a brief note from an old friend on the *Encyclopedia* staff. Its most memorable line was, "At least nobody can say that age has mellowed *you*."

Two years later, however, I again heard from the editor. His letter said, "We eat crow. We want the best article on historiography we can get, and we think you are the right man to do it." There was more, including another editorial directive. This time the latter was only a three-point program. It defined the assignment: to write in 7,000 words the history of history writing in the Western world approximately from Herodotus to David Potter, including its relation to the social sciences. My reply indicated no interest in undertaking such a job but instead proposed a parley on *Encyclopedia* turf. The parley took place a week later in the editorial office of the *Encyclopedia* with the editor-in-chief and two of his staff. After introductions and an exchange of irrelevant amenities, I opened the business at hand by putting the editor's letter on the table.

"Now about that 'best article on historiography' that you want me to write; how many who you thought were the right man to do it turned you down before you wrote me? Five?"

The advantage of a sudden verbal onslaught on a man not trained to unremitting mendacity is that it sometimes catches him with his candor showing.

"No," the editor answered, "Only three."

"And they turned you down because they would not undertake to write the history of history writing for the past 2,500 years in 7,000 words. Much less relate it to the social sciences."

He allowed that was about the situation.

"And now you are two years from deadline, and you have no general article on historiography lined up."

He allowed that this, too, was a fair précis of the situation.

"Then it begins to look like the trouble is with the directive, and that if you want an article you will have to abandon it."

The editor said that he had by now about come to that conclusion.

Having got that far, I indicated that I had no abiding interest in historiography as the history of history writing, but that I did have an interest in the writing of history as a significant form of intellectual activity, that in fact I intended to write a book about it. I planned to do a preliminary sketch, a trial run, before writing the book, and if the *Encyclopedia* wanted to look at it. . . . Anyhow it did not matter one way or the other to me since that was the direction I was going anyhow. No need for the editor to commit himself now. Just drop me a line sometime. Goodbye. . . .

Two weeks later a note arrived, "We give you *carte blanche.*" Reply: 'Who can refuse a *carte* so *blanche?*" Result: "The Rhetoric of History," as it appeared in the *Encyclopedia* three years

ago and as it appears in this volume, 21,000 words long, three
times the 7,000 called for in the initial editorial prescript. Probable moral: do not give out *cartes* quite as *blanches* as that. As a
consequence of the initial submissiveness and the subsequent per-
missiveness and generosity of the editors, the subject HISTORIOG-
RAPHY in the *Encyclopedia* is rather oddly arrayed. In alphabeti-
cal order there are articles on African, Chinese, Islamic, Japanese,
and South and Southeast Asia historiography but none on Greek,
Roman, Judaic, European, North American or Latin American
historiography. On the vast body of historical writing born of the
Western tradition in three millenia there is only silence.

It is as well that it should be so. It is doubtful that within the
allotted space anything could have been offered but a mass of
generalities at once vapid and turgid. By and large, social scientists are already disaffected to thinking about history as a way of
knowing. The article the editors thought they wanted could only
have enhanced the disaffection, persuading some social scientists
that it told them all they needed to know about the history of
history writing, persuading others that there was nothing worth
knowing. "The Rhetoric of History" may have annoyed such
social scientists, but it may also have irritated a few of them into
thinking seriously about history as professional historians write
it. At least I hope so.

That is what all the essays in this book are about, what they
have in common. They are about the profession of history and
professional history as professional historians write it, and the
author is a professional historian and a writer of professional history. Professional history is history written by men who have been
subjected to fairly rigorous training in historical research and
historical writing or who have subjected themselves to such training. In most countries this almost always involves working toward
and acquiring a post graduate degree, in the United States the
degree of Ph.D. England is an exception. There the degree structure is less rigid, although the demands of professionalism are no

less rigorous. I have a generally low opinion of amateur historians and history written by amateurs. This might be ascribed to a vested interest in professionalism. Such an ascription would be persuasive, however, only if advocacy of professionalism conferred some continuing material or psychic benefits upon the advocate which in this instance it does not. It would be even more persuasive if it were possible to point to more than a half-dozen books in English written during the past half century in my field of specialization, Europe 1450–1660, by amateurs that equalled in competence hundreds of books written in that time span by professionals. It is not possible.

So I am not only a professional historian. I am an amateur of professional history, a professional-history buff. For years I have preferred reading professional history to reading anything else, except, for recreation and relaxation, detective stories. I find this hard to believe, but it is true. It is not the sort of thing that one with a decent respect for the opinions of mankind admits. It is certainly not the sort of thing that one who casually and accidentally has drifted into associate membership in bad standing of the Eastern Intellectual Establishment admits.[1]

It would be easy enough to say that my favorite reading is the Bible, Shakespeare, Marx, and Freud. The fact, however, is that I have not yet read the Epistle to the Ephesians or the Epistles of James and Peter (although some day I intend to), or *Timon of Athens* or *The Winter's Tale* (and I never intend to). I have never read all the way through even the first volume of *Capital*, and although years ago I read most of the pieces by Freud in the old Modern Library Giant, I skipped a few, and I have not gone back to them. Yet all these books are on my shelf at home. But now, in the evening when my hand reaches out for a book and opens it, my eyes find themselves looking at Roland Mousnier's *La plume, la faucille, et le marteau*. It is a free choice. I do not really *have* to read Mousnier's collection of studies. Not reading it only adds one more book to a long list that, as I blithely and unabashedly confess to my students, I have not read. At my age one learns not to abash very easily about such delinquencies. In this matter it seems to me that the hand and eyes are a more honest and reliable index to one's preferences than the spoken avowal.

So I am an amateur of professional history. I cherish it, day to day, care more for it than I care for the greatest achievements of the greatest minds of the past. This is not to assert, of course, that I think professional history is better than Shakespeare or Freud, much less that Roland Mousnier, able historian though he is, is better. On many or most conceivable scales of competence, imagination, and intellectual force Mousnier would rank whole universes below Shakespeare and Freud, or would not belong in the scale at all. But on the scale of professional historians, Mousnier stands pretty high. He does skillfully the things professional historians need to know how to do.

What continues, after all these years, to fascinate me about professionals is not the vast overarching insights they achieve. They usually don't, and they rarely even try. A professional historian does not often dedicate a work to "the march of civilization—in broad outline as it were—and the civilizing forces of the future."[2] He leaves such heroics to the Eilert Lövbergs of the day who usually attain a fast professional suicide in the rackety stews of current intellectual chic. What I love to watch the skillful pro do is make those easy-looking but difficult right moves that, whatever the situation may be, distinguish the winners from the losers. Lawrence Stone rendering visible the deterioration of the social value of aristocratic status in early seventeenth-century England by tracing the fall in the market value of titles of honor. Roland Mousnier detecting the hostility of regional France to the royal center in noble incitement and support of peasant revolts against the king's tax collectors. Edmund Morgan tracing the topography of old and current local feuds in the alignment of opposition to and support of the mother country in the Stamp Act crisis. Garrett Mattingly making sense of Elizabeth I's refusal to risk the English fleet in a venture against Spain early in the year of the Armada not only through her reflexive penuriousness, but also through the effect of a hard winter in the North Atlantic on the subsequent battle readiness of the fleet and the health or mere survival of the crews. Sir John Neale, by the masterly mobilization of a few scraps of evidence, reversing a venerable judgment on the extent to which the initial settlement of the English Church in 1559 was the work of the virgin queen.

The elegant, economical response of a historian to his evidence that makes professional history watching my favorite intellectual pastime is not confined to the old pros. Occasionally one finds it even in that much maligned exercise, the doctoral dissertation. I think of Erik Midelfort's study of witch-hunting in South West Germany. In each peaking of the craze, Midelfort traces with meticulous care the spread of accusations until it begins to reach the families of the magistrates and the magistrates themselves. Then the wave recedes. Men perceive that to continue to believe charges of witchcraft in the particular instance at hand will erode the entire structure of the community. So they cease to believe that this time the particular persons accused are really witches. Since, however, the rejection of witchcraft is particular—this time, here, now, these people—the soil of belief is still fertile, and in propitious circumstances brings forth a new witchcraft craze.

And I think of Brian Levack's equally meticulous study of a small cluster of Englishmen—the lawyers who made their living from the practice of civil law rather than common law from the accession of James I to 1640. What Levack presents is a nearly perfect instance of the determination of political attitude by vocational choice. He explores the whole surviving record of the conditions of livelihood and life of each of the civil lawyers. When he is done, he has demonstrated beyond doubt that those conditions, not the supposed predilection of Roman civil law for absolutism, turned the civil lawyers into supporters of Church and monarchy when Englishmen in almost every other vocation were souring on both.

For me, clearly the satisfactions of an amateur of professional history are intensified and deepened by my own professionalism. I know the difference between being a professional amateur and being an amateur amateur, because with respect to baseball I am the latter. When I see John Bench of the Cincinnati Reds make a perfect throw from his catcher's crouch to nail a fast runner trying to steal second, I know I have seen a superb performance. I know it because most of the other catchers I have seen have to rise out of their crouch to make such a throw and thus lose the fraction of a second that is often the difference between cutting the runner down and having him reach base safe. But I do not know it the way someone who has played the position of catcher a while knows it. I do not know what it is like to have to catch a baseball behind home plate and throw it about 127 feet on a line so it will come in just where the second baseman can catch it and tag the runner from first sliding into the base, a runner who has moved about a quarter of his 90-foot run even before the pitcher has released the ball. I do not know it in my hands and arm and eye, in all my mind and bones and muscles.

It is in this empathetic way that I perceive a skillful historical account. I am not taken in, as I sometimes am in baseball, by the grandstand player who makes himself look good to an amateur and bad to a professional by making an easy play look hard. Neither a flood of statistics by a "scientific" historian nor a gush of words by a "literary" one distracts my attention from the historical moves they are trying to make and from the wasteful, inept way they have taken to make them. I usually have a notion of what another historian is up to, of whether he has managed his data like a pro or like a dub,* because I have had to work with

---

* Not always a clear notion, of course, if the time, place, and subject are remote from the ones I am familiar with. Then I will not know whether the historian in question has been efficient and imaginative in his search of the record of the past for data. I will only be able to judge his skill in deploying the data he actually uses.

records of the past, too. Often enough I have done it in a mediocre way, but I have done it well a few times, well enough to have a feel for what doing it well entails.

This capacity for a total appreciative response to solid, substantial and elegant historical craftsmanship which is based on one's own occasional achievement of such craftsmanship is a true pleasure, but, alas! it is a mixed one. In the nature of his vocation a professional historian has to read a great deal of history. And a great deal of that great deal is botched work. The tiny kernels of insight, perception, and discovery in much of the work of many professional historians are buried in thick, heavy shells of incompetence, dullness, and confusion. It is disturbing that this should be so. The pride I take in my profession is diminished by the sense that many historians practice it in a way which, were they physicians, would lose them their license—heedlessly, thoughtlessly, irresponsibly. Any historian who has served as an editorial adviser for historical journals knows that the sludge which fills so many pages of such journals is only the top of the drossberg. And what is, as it were, under the water—the contributions the advisers turn down, the contributions that the editor rejects out of hand so that an adviser never sees them—is far more dreary than the stuff that gets into print.

Yet practically all of it, the bad that gets published and the worse that does not, is the work of professional historians. That is, it is the work of men and women who, after four years in college during which they usually majored in history, have spent four to six years in intensive graduate training to earn the standard certification of professional competence, the degree of Doctor of Philosophy in history. When one considers the length of the training period in conjunction with the manifest inability of many of those who have met the training requirements to write history competently and skillfully, those responsible for training professional historians are obliged to say, "We must be doing *something* wrong."

Very nearly all the history I read has been written in the present century. That does not mean that I think all the good history has been written in the last seventy years. With respect to the tract of the past which as a professional historian I know most about, Western Europe from 1400 to 1660, I do have a hunch that of the professional history I enjoy, the greater part has been written during that time. This is hardly surprising. In the Western world there has probably been more history written since 1900 than during the entire span of earlier centuries, and the notion of history as an academic discipline and a profession does not go much further back of 1900 than the present day stands beyond it. Some of the founding fathers, Ranke and Burckhardt for example, were men of such extraordinary skill, perceptiveness, and dedication to honest judgment that it is still both exciting and instructive to watch them move about the historical terrain in which they were the first comers. Nevertheless, A. F. Pollard, Sir John Neale, and Garrett Mattingly wrote better history about the Tudor period than did James Anthony Froude, Georges Lefevre wrote better history about the French Revolution than Michelet or Carlyle, and Mousnier wrote better history about the age of Louis XIV than Voltaire.

This superiority of the professional historians who wrote in the twentieth century is in part due to the enhanced rigor of their training, in part to the more ready accessibility to them of large deposits of historical evidence and of techniques of dealing with it, in part to the preparatory work of precisely such pioneers as Froude, Michelet, and Voltaire. A similar situation exists, for example, in track. In 1915 N. S. Taher held the official world record for the mile—four minutes, 12.6 seconds. In 1967, Jim Ryun ran a mile in three minutes, 51.1 seconds. He was able to do it partly because the track was better, partly because he was put through better training, and partly because more is known now than in 1915 about how to run a mile fast. The same situation holds in cookery. Meals at a great restaurant in 1970 are probably better than their equivalent in 1850 would have been. The ingredients are often of higher quality, more varied, and more reliable, the *batterie de cuisine is* more sophisticated, the rules are more precise, and the training is more exacting.

Compared with history, however, cookery is in some respects an advanced skill. In cookery I am not a professional, only a fairly practiced amateur. Yet I can prepare, indeed have prepared, a *caneton bigarade* that tastes as good as what one would get in a first-rate restaurant in Paris. Although any apprentice in the kitchen of a good restaurant could rightly fault me for my *inefficiency* in preparing the duckling and its sauce, he would have to give me good marks on the final product. Thus while in broad expertise I am pitifully inferior to the chef of the Relais Gastronomique de Paris-Est, with respect to what appears on the diner's plate when he orders *caneton bigarade* I am that great chef's equal.

What is true of cookery is not true of history. Many historians long trained in the craft, not amateurs but professionals, have never produced and will never produce twenty pages of history as good as *any consecutive twenty* in the work of Maitland, or Mattingly, or Bloch, or even—to drop a hundred rungs on the ladder—me.

There are a good many reasons why this should be so. The ingredients of *caneton bigarade* are always much alike—similar constituents in similar proportions; not the identical orange peel, the identical duckling, the identical carmelized vinegar and sugar, of course, but so nearly alike as to make little difference. Not so in history. The record of the Gordon riots in London in 1780 is not very much like that of the Birmingham riots in 1791; Hobbes' *Leviathan* is a far cry from Plato's *Republic*; and both are a far cry from Rousseau's *Social Contract*. One would do poorly by the past to render an account of riots or treatises by the application of a standard formula. Nevertheless, given an equivalent familiarity with the record, to have written a good historical account of one riot or one political treatise should (and I think does) improve a historian's chances of writing a good account of another riot or another treatise. Indeed, on the face of the evidence it is clear that a historian who has written one good historical account of almost anything is more likely to write another of almost anything he chooses than is a historian who has written only a bad historical account. And this at least suggests that the writer of consistently good historical accounts *knows* something about writing history that the writer of bad ones does not know. It also points to the possibility that he could communicate what he knows.

And here professional history is deficient, just where cookery is excellently equipped. In the kitchen in our house there are twenty-odd cookbooks. A half-dozen at least have instructions for *caneton bigarade*. Two of them are probably but not certainly worthless. Not that the authors are bad chefs. They may be good chefs but they are bad writers of cookbooks, as I already know by unfortunate experience. The instructions for preparing *caneton bigarade* in the other four books are not identical. Yet no matter which of the four recipes I follow, I will end with an admirable duckling in orange sauce.

In history there are no equivalents of Craig Claiborne's *New York Times Cookbook,* or Julia Child's *Mastering the Art of French Cooking,* or Irma Rombauer's *Joy of Cooking.* For some reason when they write about history writing, historians, including me, usually concern themselves with historiography (that is, the history of history writing), or the theory of historical knowledge (causation, explanation, relativism, and so on), or methods of finding records and evaluating them for veracity and accuracy. Only in this last sort of manual do historians approach the kind of guidance that a good cookbook provides, and then not very close. Such manuals are less like cookbooks than like instructions for shopping for the ingredients one needs in order to start cooking, with cautionary notes on how to check for adulteration and how to avoid being poisoned by what happens to turn up on the market. That is all very well, worthy, and necessary. Unfortunately, however, instruction tends to stop just at the point where the problems of chopping, paring, slicing, and blending the ingredients begin—how much of what? what should be rapid-boiled down and concentrated? what simmered slowly? what skimmed off or strained out and discarded? That is to say, the manual usually stops just where the actual operation of writing history starts.

It goes without saying that good historians know how to perform the complicated operations of judgment, of incorporation or rejection of data, of ordering of and emphasis on evidence that enable them to write good history. Knowing how to perform such operations is indispensible to writing good history. But it is not at all clear that historians know how they perform them. It is even less clear whether they could give a coherent account of how they perform them; and it is not certain that a series of such accounts would be useful in the way that good cookbooks are useful. The analogy between cooking and history writing is too loose to warrant excessive optimism.

And yet . . . And yet our present methods of transmitting the skills of our craft are inordinately hit-or-miss and wasteful. The very able graduate student who recently told me that he had learned nothing useful to him in the courses he took in graduate school may have underestimated their worth or may have been the victim of exceptional circumstances. I do not think—I would rather not think—that none of the earnest sufferers in all my history seminars gained anything for their pains. Yet that some gained almost nothing I am quite sure; of that the evidence of their seminar papers persuades me against my will. Some, I suppose, could never have been taught; their gifts were too meager. When all is said and done, writing history is a more complicated and perplexing skill than cooking. Others, however, learned to write history with more pain and less ease than they might have. Without experience, prescription, I know, is not enough; but it is possible that thoughtful, systematic prescription would take some of the edge of anguish from the experience of the novices, make them better historians faster, and turn them toward rather than away from that writing of history which has been to me so fulfilling a vocation.

To set among its distant corporate goals the exploration of ways to transmit more effectively than we do the rudiments of our art would not be unworthy of the profession to which I am proud to belong. History stands sorely in need of a pedagogic equivalent of *The Joy of Cooking*.[3]

2 /

The Rhetoric of History

EREIN, the word "historiography" will be taken to mean
the craft of writing history and/or the yield of such writing considered in its rhetorical aspect. The term "history" will be used to describe the study of the past as a systematic discipline. It will not be used to refer to the past as such. Unnecessary ambiguities created by using the term "history" to identify both the past and the systematic study of it have occasionally led to gratuitous confusion. The terms "historiography," "the rhetoric of history," and "history writing" will be used as synonyms. Historiography is different from the collection of historical evidence, the editing of historical sources, the exercise of historical thought and imagination, the criticism of historical writing, and the philosophy of history, but it is related to all of them and overlaps some of them. It is also different from the history of history writing. This distinction must be kept in mind because in recent decades the term "historiography" has increasingly been used to mean the history of history writing—in effect, a branch of intellectual history or a subbranch of the sociology of knowledge. It will not be used in that sense here.

Perhaps the drift of the term "historiography" from its

initial moorings of meaning resulted from the neglect of systematic study of the rhetoric of history and from the view,
usually implicit rather than explicit, that that rhetoric is not
specific to history, or not specific enough to warrant systematic
study; for if the rhetoric of history is generic rather than specific,
then historiography so defined has no separate identity and
merges into general rhetoric. Although many historians have
said wise and witty things about the writing of history, none has
focused more than intermittent attention on the problems it
raises. The casualness with which historians have investigated
the structure of historiography, compared with the care and
exacting scrutiny to which they subject the nature of data, evidence, and inference in works of history, indicates that in their
role as critics they regard the latter as the historians' legitimate
central preoccupation and the former as a secondary and independent matter in which excellence, although desirable, is dispensable and without effect on the validity of the finished work.

To test this implied judgment—which is very hard to recon-
cile with the care and pains which many of the best historians
lavish on their own history writing—this article will attempt an
analysis of historiography.

The models of history writing that will be dealt with will
be those provided in recent times by the better historians in
their better moments. "In recent times" because, although the
writing of history is old, the *general* professional commitment
of historians *always* to write it with the maximum verisimilitude
to the past is relatively new—scarcely 150 years old. The focus
will be on "the better historians in their better moments" because they should and often do set the standards at which the
profession aims. It is the practice of these historians when
actually writing history, not their explicit theoretical or quasi-
philosophical views, that is of concern here; for it is in their
practice of historiography rather than in peripheral excursions
into the problems of methodology that they reveal their effective
commitments. Although much that follows will apply to all

historiography, the article is only incidentally concerned with historical writings intended to codify knowledge of history already available, such as textbooks; primarily it is focused on history writing aimed at extending the bounds of historical knowledge. Since historiography communicates what the historian knows or thinks he knows, a consideration of the historian's way of writing that does not relate it to his way of knowing is doomed to triviality. Finally, as an overarching principle this article will seek to relate the rhetoric of history to the rhetoric of the mathematizing natural sciences, taking physics and chemistry as models, in order to make clear the similarities of historiography to these other ways in which men seek to communicate what they think they know, and its differences from them.

The language of historians

The most cursory comparison of any professional journal of history with an issue of the *Physical Review* will carry the conviction that the rhetoric of history differs grossly from that of physics. Ideally the vocabulary of physics is exact and denotative, and its syntax is mathematical, expressing quantitative relations between entities defined with the minimum ambiguity possible, given the current state of knowledge of the science. Now a part of the distinctive vocabulary of historiography is also denotative and unambiguous—the terms "pipe roll" or "writ of trespass" no less so, for example, than the term "specific gravity," although most if not all of the vocabulary of history that is at once distinctive and unambiguous is likely to refer to universes more constricted in time and space or less homogeneous and uniform than the ones the vocabulary of physics refers to. Moreover, historians often use quantitative data: grain yields per acre, rates of population growth, average rainfall; and sometimes they employ the syntax of mathematics to determine such matters as median income, ratio of cargo weight to number of sailors, range of probable error in equating number of manors owned with gross income from land. Thus, they occasionally mathematize, they often quantify and enumerate, and part of their vocabulary is wholly denotative. When operating in a sector of history writing where they deem rhetorical devices of this sort alone to be appropriate, they assimilate the form of their vocabulary very closely to that of the natural sciences and exercise a like care to decontaminate it of connotative and evocative overtones. Yet very few historians consistently write history this way, and scarcely any of that very few would insist that *all* history ought to aim at the rhetoric of the natural sciences as an ideal goal; they do not seek to make the rhetorical form which they find convenient into a prescriptive rule for the entire profession, as they would be obligated to do if they thought that *only* with such a rhetoric could one come close to an account of things past that approaches maximum verisimilitude.

In this respect historians differ notably from many social scientists. Both historians and social scientists claim, as natural scientists do, that by their method of investigation and formulation appropriately applied, they are able to produce cumulative increments to men's knowledge. Both historians and social scientists acknowledge that the form of their rhetoric is not always coincident with that of the natural sciences. But since most social scientists take the rhetoric of the natural sciences as their goal and ideal, they make a major intellectual effort to assimilate their way of writing to that of the natural sciences. In this matter they regard any nonconformity on their part as a deformity, to be either overcome or lamented. In practice, historians rarely see historiographic problems in this light. Far from always seeking the forms of language which will enable them to make historiography into the closest possible replica of the language of the natural sciences, they choose—often unself-consciously, but sometimes well aware of what they are doing—to write in a way that the rhetoric of the sciences forecloses. They deliberately choose a word or a phrase that is imprecise and may turn out to be ambiguous, because of its rich aura of connotation. Without compunction they sacrifice exactness for evocative force. Since the only common purpose to which historians are bound by their calling to commit themselves is to advance understanding of the past, the only possible justification for such a sacrifice is that it serves to increase knowledge of the past, that sometimes an evocative rhetoric is the best means a historian has for formulating and communicating what he knows. Whether or not the historians who in practice follow this rhetorical strategy are fully aware of it, the implication of this strategy is very radical. It entails the claim that historians can produce cumulative increments of knowledge without consistent resort to the rhetoric which scientists have found indispensable for formulating and communicating what they know. Positively it implies that for communicating what the historian knows, a rhetoric more like that employed in the fictive arts than like that employed in the sciences is not only permissible but on occasion indispensable.

Knowing and communicating

To analyze historiography, we must first determine its place in the general process of knowing and communicating. In order to identify and comprehend this general process, we will start with a concrete proposition: Willie Mays knows baseball. To deny this proposition is to fly in the face of the unamimous and considered judgment of several million people who have seen Mays play ball. Alternatively, it is to restrict the meaning of the term "know" so drastically as to impede the flow of discourse and snarl up a channel of communication. For a man who can convince some five million observers out of five million, and his employers to the tune of a salary of $125,000 per year, that he knows has come as close to ironclad demonstration as one can get in matters involving human judgment. To generate this conviction, Mays employs the rhetoric of action, the most common and universal method of demonstrating that one knows.

(The author realizes that he is rather stretching the common sense of the term "rhetoric" in the present context.) The adequacy of such demonstration is measured by consistent appropriateness of visible (or perceivable) response. Briefly, Willie Mays shows that he knows by what he does. While he demonstrates almost perfectly *that* he knows, for two reasons he would have great difficulty in saying how he knows what he knows. (1) Since much of what he knows is in the area of action, he probably knows no way of putting it into words. (2) Much of what he knows, he knows from long experience, and although some of what he knows in this way can be rendered accessible in verbal form, and is known by others in that form, that is not in fact how *he* knows it. If we went further and insisted that he so exactly communicate in words what he knows that others could test its validity by replication, we would clearly be asking the impossible, because he does not know what he knows with some abstraction from himself called his discursive intellect but with his whole person; and in every game he plays, he demonstrates its validity, not by verbal or mathematical formulation but by the unique and unreplicable perfection of his response.

In one area of human knowing, investigation in the natural sciences, however, formal convention has established as a minimal evidence of knowing the ability to state the results in a wholly denotative rhetoric of verbal signs; all consistently appropriate responses are required ultimately to assume this form. This convention has been adopted because scientists set a very high value on generalizability of statement, replicability of experiment, and logical entailment as tests of knowing; and the rhetoric they have chosen enforces entailment and makes generalization and replication possible with maximum efficiency and certainty. Scientists have no doubt adopted this particular rhetorical stratagem because they have found it very useful for eliciting and testing answers to the kinds of questions they habitually ask. Correlatively, however, it prevents them, as scientists, from asking questions that are recalcitrant to formulation in the rhetoric they have chosen, and a fortiori from answering such questions. As a result of this set of circumstances, in the sciences it is by definition meaningless to say that one knows or understands a result, a law, or a hypothesis but cannot state or communicate what one thus claims to understand. If I cannot state the binomial theorem, or the law of inverse squares, or the valence rule, I do not know it, and any claim to the contrary is simply nonsense. In effect, the strategy of the sciences in the codification of their results is to reduce to a minimum in practice and to nothing in theory the gap between cognition and written communication.

The range of knowing, then, extends from what Willie Mays knows about baseball, which we would accept as demonstrated whether or not Mays can put together a single coherent sentence on the subject, to what a physicist knows about the results of investigations in physics, which he can demonstrate only with a denotative vocabulary and a mathematical syntax. The common factor is the capacity of each to render a consistently appropriate response; the difference lies in the nature of the response that is deemed appropriate; and the criterion of appropriateness is efficacy in encompassing the purpose of the activity to which the actor has committed himself.

In this general setting of the relation between knowing and communicating, what is the relation between knowing history and its communication in writing, that is, historiography? In the first place, among professional historians there is a rough consensus about the responses appropriate for writers of history when they set out to communicate what they know. This consensus enables one to speak of "the better historians" with a sense that one's judgment is not merely personal, random, or arbitrary. The consensus is approximately registered by the price a particular historian fetches in the current job market. (Only approximately, however, since a number of items other than the profession's estimate of his history writing go to make his price—his age, his reputed aptitude in face-to-face teaching, his personal qualities, the relation of supply to demand in his special field of interest, and so on.) Second, in writing history, as we have seen, some historians consistently use a vocabulary and a syntax similar to those which are standard in the natural sciences and some do not. There is, however, no significant correlation between the list of those who do so and the list of "better historians." This implies that in historiography, historians do not accept the scientists' conception of what constitutes a consistently appropriate response in the public presentation of the results of scientific investigation. An inquiry of no very pressing sort would reveal that in practice they have refused fully to commit themselves to a scientific rhetoric because they concern themselves with questions and answers which are not wholly tractable to the kind of formulation that scientists aim at, and because they assume in practice a relationship between cognition and communication in history different from that which is currently acceptable in the sciences.

Historians acquire their command of the data that they ultimately deploy in writing history through reading and considering what men have written in the past and about the past and by giving attention to remnants and traces of men's handiwork surviving from the past: buildings, tools, pictures, field systems, tombs, pots—archeological data in the broadest sense, The process of learning starts in a haphazard way with the student's earliest interest in history, and for the professional historian becomes more systematic and more sharply focused in the course of his training. In general, the training of a historian aims at the complementary but sometimes conflicting goals of simultaneously extending the range of his knowledge and of bringing it intensively to bear on some limited constellation of past happenings, in writing about which he is expected to make some contribution to the advancement of historical knowledge.

This process of knowing which goes on throughout the historian's active professional life is not identical with the knowing through experience which enables most men to meet most of the contingencies of their days on earth without continual bafflement, frustration, and disaster; but it is similar to it. It is not identical because in some measure the historian chooses what he will confront, while much of what men know through day-to-day experience comes at them haphazardly by no choice of their own.

Second, the layman's kind of knowledge is in large part acquired through face-to-face confrontation with persons and situations, while the historian's confrontation with men and situations of the past is mainly (in most cases, wholly) indirect, mediated by the surviving documentary and archeological record. Nevertheless, the difference ought not to be exaggerated, for there is considerable overlap. The printing press and more recent media of communication have vastly extended the role of indirect confrontation in day-to-day experiential knowledge. Moreover, in his quest for understanding of the past, the historian relies to a considerable extent on the cautious and qualified analogical application of experiential knowledge which he has accumulated in personal, face-to-face transactions during his own lifetime.

Finally, the difference between face-to-face confrontation and confrontation mediated by the historical record is one of mode but not necessarily of quality, or intensity, or depth, or coherence, or completeness. Any man who reads and meditates on the twelve volumes of the correspondence of Desiderius Erasmus, extending over a span of four decades, plus his massive literary output, may justly argue that in quality, intensity, depth, coherence, and completeness his experiential knowledge of that sixteenth-century intellectual, acquired through mediated confrontation, is more firmly based than the experiential knowledge that any contemporary of Erasmus had of him. Indeed, it is as firmly based as the knowledge available today about any intellectual now living. The similarity between the two kinds of knowledge we have been considering is that for many purposes the consistently appropriate response which indicates their presence is not and need not be verbal, and when verbal, it need not and quite possibly cannot take the form of wholly denotative statement, much less of mathematical formulation. For such purposes it lies closer to the Willie Mays pole of response by effective action than to the scientific pole of response by communicating results in unambiguous statement.

In a large part of his work, the historian has no need at all for such statement or for any coherent verbal statement at all. He is massively engaged in finding out what happened and how it happened. To do these things he must formulate rough hypotheses, often very rough, about what happened and how it happened, and then examine the available record to verify or correct his hypotheses. But at the outset, from an almost limitless range of conceivable hypotheses he must select for investigation the very few that lie somewhere in the target area; he must select only those for which the surviving records hold forth some hope of verification; and he must have a sense of what records among a multitude are likely to provide the evidence he needs. A historian unable to do any of these things would remain an inept novice all his life. Relying on their knowledge of the past, historians successfully do these things day after day, yet most of them would be at a loss to explain their particular choices. They tend to ascribe their general aptitude for making better rather than worse choices to "knowing the ropes" and "having been around a long time in this period." In effect, the knowledge that a historian relies on for a very considerable part of his work is experiential and results from a long and extensive familiarity with the historical record. (There is a legitimate doubt whether much of the foregoing does not apply as readily to the actual work of scientists as to that of historians.) For the historian the link between knowing and communicating is loose and weak; on the basis of his own experience of this looseness, he inclines to give some, if not full, faith and credit to colleagues who claim to know about the past much that they cannot adequately express in writing. Communication through historiography requires historians to put into written words what they know experientially and diffusely about the past, to organize it into coherent and sequential statements in order to make it fully accessible first to themselves and then to others. Their communication with others, the history they end up writing, thus starts four removes from the episodes in the past that concern them. Between the two lie the historical record, the historians' experiential knowledge acquired through their exploration of that record, and their attempts to communicate to themselves what they know.

Through these interposed layers historians, in and by their writing, seek, along with many other things, to enable their readers to follow the movement and to sense the tempo of events; to grasp and do justice to the motives and actions of men; to discern the imperatives that move men to action; and to distinguish those imperatives from the pseudo imperatives that have become mere exercises in pious ejaculation; to recognize the impact on the course of events of an accident, a catastrophe, or a bit of luck; and to be aware of what the participants in a struggle conceived the stakes to be. (This particular set of items which historians sometimes feel called on to communicate through the three layers has purposely been selected because (1) none of them are explanatory in the scientific sense and (2) none can be effectively communicated in a purely scientific rhetoric.) The historian's ability both as an investigator of the past and as a writer of history is measured negatively by the extent to which he lets the layers that intervene between the episode in the past and the reader of his work insulate the reader from the past, positively by the extent to which he is able to make these layers serve as a conductor of knowledge of the past to his readers. Historians give faith and credit to their fellows who protest that they know and yet confess that they cannot communicate what they know, because in some measure every historian is aware how far he has failed in his writing of history to penetrate those layers in his effort to communicate what he knows of the past.

Given this sense of the inadequacy of their use of language to their task, historians would surely welcome as an alternative a wholly denotative universal vocabulary which would narrow to a scarcely discernible crevice the perilous chasm that for them separates cognition from communication and sets them ransacking the whole storehouse of their mother tongue instead of relying on a manageable number of well-designed symbolic structures to overcome it. The fact that no such alternative adequate to communicate what historians know about the past has up to now emerged suggests that the relation between knowing the past and the writing of history is such as to preclude that alternative, that in practice historians believe that the sacrifice of the knowledge of the past which it would entail renders inappropriate the universal imposition in historiography of the denotative rhetoric of scientific discourse.

Of course historians can avoid their rhetorical difficulties (1) by attempting to communicate about the past only that knowledge which can be expressed in a rhetoric nearly like that of the natural sciences or (2) by attempting to know about the past only what can be so communicated. In fact, historians have pursued both these courses. Some historians have taken the first course either because of a special interest in the sorts of historical problems manageable within the confines of a quasi-scientific rhetoric or because their special aptitude for that rhetoric has turned their attention to the sorts of problem with which it can deal. Others have taken the second course either out of allegiance to a conception (or misconception) called scientific history or because by calling their thinking and writing about the past scientific history, they thought they could sanctify their incompetence and dullness.

On the whole, however, historians have not been willing to truncate their knowledge of the past to fit the special aptitudes of a few historians or the misconceptions or painful ineptitude of a number of others. Instead, to make their experiential knowledge of the past accessible to readers who cannot recapitulate the processes by which that knowledge was acquired, they have used almost every device of rhetoric compatible with their commitment to a clear and intelligible presentation of the evidence on which their knowledge is based. That the language they use is frequently evocative and even metaphorical and that much of its vocabulary is not that of scientific demonstration but of the ordinary discourse of educated men, testifies to their conviction—rarely explicit, sometimes not wholly conscious—that these are the appropriate means for bringing their readers into that confrontation with events long past and men long dead which is an indispensable condition of knowing them. To the extent that the historian's rhetoric falls short of communicating what he believes he has discovered about the past, what he thinks he knows does not become generally available and cannot be tested publicly by other historians. To that extent, therefore, there is a loss of potential knowledge of the past. Conversely, to the extent that he succeeds in communicating anything that hitherto he alone has known, there is gain. Therefore, the advancement of historical knowledge depends to a considerable extent on the quality of the historian's rhetoric, on the efficacy of his historiography, and is almost inseparable from it; far from impeding the advancement of historical knowledge, language evocative rather than wholly denotative in intent and character becomes a means and a condition of that advancement.

Modes of explanation

Historiography is the means for communicating in writing what the historian thinks he knows about the past. Efficient and effective communication requires him, in writing history, to array what he knows according to some principle of coherence. The principle of coherence traditionally and still most generally employed by historians is narrative. Usually, but not always, they communicate what they know by telling a story or stories. Despite its venerable antiquity, narrative has recently come under attack as a means for providing coherence in history. The most general ground for attack seems to be the contention that the coherence it provides is nonexplanatory or inadequately explanatory. In this respect it is compared invidiously with the principle of coherence by subsumption under general laws supposedly standard in the rhetoric of the sciences, which is said to provide adequate explanation. If subsumption under general laws is the principle of coherence standard in the sciences, if by the criteria of the sciences it alone provides adequate explanation, and if the provision of adequate explanation is the sole or prime function of the sciences, then clearly narrative does *not* meet the scientific standard of coherence, nor does it provide adequate scientific explanation. It remains to ask, however, why historians should prefer a principle of coherence and criteria of explanatory adequacy borrowed from the rhetoric of the sciences both to narrative, their own traditional principle of coherence, and to the view of the nature and conditions of historical explanation which their use of narrative implies.

The ascription of adequacy to explanations of the general-law type seems to be based on both aesthetic and practical considerations. (1) Elegance, precision, clarity, internal consistency, and structural tidiness—a place for everything and everything in its place—in the domain of knowing: all these are aesthetically attractive concomitants of general-law explanations and are the generator and the justification of the denotative vocabulary and the mathematical syntax at which scientists aim. (2) In many or most cases, such explanations afford scientists the opportunity to replicate the experiment that was offered as evidence of the applicability of the general law, and thus to test the validity either of the law or of its application. (3) The rhetoric of the sciences facilitates the rapid and efficient identification of new problems and problem areas. (4) The expansion of the range and precision of general-law explanations has roughly coincided on the temporal scale with an extraordinary expansion of man's control of vast tracts of his environment over which hitherto he had exercised no control at all. Although by the general-law canon, or indeed by any canon of explanation that has not been in disrepute since Aristotle, such a coincidence taken alone does *not* adequately explain the expansion of control, still nothing succeeds like success, and the aura of prestige acquired by the natural sciences in the past three centuries has rubbed off on the criteria of adequate explanation ascribed to them, especially in the eyes of intellectually insecure social scientists and historians.

No one has ever made clear why the criteria of adequate explanation acceptable to scientists in their work should also be acceptable to historians in theirs, or why adequacy of explanation should be the *sole* criterion of consistently appropriate response for the historian engaged in the work of communicating his knowledge in writing. Adequacy of explanation is clearly relative to that which is to be explained. A guidebook to a city, for example, explains the location of a "point of interest" by designating what streets it is on and nearest to and by indicating the means of access to it from other points by various means of transportation. A real estate survey explains its location by designating the frontage and depth of the lot, the street it faces on, and the distance of the lot from the nearest intersecting street. Both explanations are accurate, exact enough for their respective purposes, and therefore adequate; each communicates the knowledge likely to be sought by one particular sort of seeker and thus provides the appropriate response to his questions; neither invokes any general law, nor need it do so; neither is a scientific explanation, nor need it be so. Moreover, the notion that the sole appropriate response of the historian to his commitment to communicate what he knows is something designated "explanation" is wildly arbitrary. It involves either consigning a large part of that response to the domain of irrelevance or so extending the meaning of "explanation" as to render it unrecognizable by scientists, philosophers, ordinary readers, and historians themselves.

HISTORICAL NARRATIVE / Narrative, which is the rhetorical mode most commonly resorted to by historians, is also their most common mode of explanation. It is not in fact scientific by the criteria just indicated; it cannot be rendered scientific because it is formally not reducible to the general-law type of explanation; and no more than the "explanations where" set forth above need it be scientific in order to be adequate, unless one insists on applying the scientific criteria of adequacy to a nonscientific explanation. Narrative is the most common mode of historical explanation because it is often the kind of explanatory answer solicited by a kind of question that historians very often ask and and that is very often asked of them. Two ordinary forms of this question are "How did it come about that . . . ?" and "How did he (or they) happen to . . . ?" For example, "How did it come about that a Labour government took power in England in 1964?" or "How did the New York Giants happen to play in the World Series in 1951?" The following discussion will be organized around a treatment of this second question. The writer has selected it because it leads quickly into so many of the topics of this section and because its evidential base is one on which he is more than ordinarily well-informed.

The call for an explanation of how the Giants happened to play in the World Series of 1951 can be so construed as to make it amenable to explanation of the general-law type.

A. *The particular facts*

1. In 1951 the New York Giants were a baseball team in the National League.

2. In 1951, during the official National League baseball season, the New York Giants won more games from the other teams in that league and lost fewer to them than any of the other teams in the league won or lost.

B. *The general law*

Whenever during the official National League season a National League team wins more games and loses fewer than any other team in that league, it plays in the World Series.[1]

The answer perfectly fulfills all the requirements of the general-law type of explanation, including denotative univocal vocabulary and strict deductive entailment. Yet from the point of view of the writer and reader of history, such an answer is patently unsatisfactory. The reason is that in the context of the National League season of 1951, the appropriate response to the question "How did the Giants happen to play in the World Series of 1951?" is the historical *story* of how the Giants came to lead the National League at the end of the official season that year. A general-law explanation cannot tell that story; indeed, it cannot tell any story. It is not built to tell stories. From this very simple instance an important conclusion follows: general law and narrative are not merely alternative but equally valid modes of explanation. In the above instance the general-law explanation does not tell the questioner what he wants to know; for him it is neither a good nor a bad, neither an adequate nor an inadequate, explanation—it is no explanation at all. And conversely, to other questioners asking scientists *and* historians for an "explanation," a response in the form of a story would be quite inappropriate and therefore no explanation at all. The validity of either mode of explanation is determined by the appropriateness and adequacy of its response to a particular question. In effect, the validity of modes of explanation is not something that exists *in vacuo,* but only in relation to what particular inquirers at particular moments seek to know.

In view of the frequent irrelevance of pure general-law explanation to past situations that require the telling of a story, attempts have been made to adapt the general-law type of explanation to narrative. Narrative explanation is usually presented as a series of statements of continuous causal linkages between events such that in the chains of causation (1) each effect is imputed to precedent causes and (2) the imputation implies either the actuality or the possibility of a general law or laws such that, taken with the precedent causes, they entail the effect.

For present purposes it is to our advantage that the official rules of baseball provide us with a vocabulary almost as purely denotative as that of the sciences. In that vocabulary we can produce a narrative explanation of how the New York Giants won the 1951 National League pennant and thus played in the World Series; this explanation conforms to the foregoing model.

National League Standings as of September 30, 1951

	Won	Lost
Brooklyn Dodgers	96	58
New York Giants	96	58

Because of the tie at the end of the regular season Brooklyn and New York were required to play additional games, the first team to win two games to be designated as the National League entry in the World Series.

First additional game, Oct. 1, 1951: final score, New York 3, Brooklyn 1; games won, New York 1, Brooklyn 0.

Second additional game, Oct. 2, 1951: final score, Brooklyn 10, New York 0; games won, New York 1, Brooklyn 1.

Third additional game, Oct. 3, 1951: inning-by-inning score to second half of the ninth inning:

Brooklyn	1	0	0	0	0	0	0	3	0
New York	0	0	0	0	0	0	1	0	

Score to second half of the ninth inning, Brooklyn 4, New York 1. New York at bat.

The first batter singled. The second batter singled. Because the first batter was a reasonably fast runner, he advanced to third base. Because the third batter hit a short fly ball which was caught, he was out. Because the fourth batter doubled, the first batter scored a run, and the second batter advanced to third base, where he was replaced by a substitute runner because he had hurt his leg. The Brooklyn pitcher was replaced because three New York players out of four had made safe hits off his pitching. Because the fifth batter hit a home run the substitute runner, the fourth batter, and the fifth batter scored runs. Because New York scored four runs in the second half of the ninth inning, making the score 5 to 4, they won the game. Because they won two games of the play-off before Brooklyn did, they won more games and lost fewer than any other team in the National League. Because of this they played in the World Series of 1951.

About the preceding narrative explanation a number of highly instructive points are worth noting.

(1) It almost perfectly conforms to the proposed structure of narrative explanation outlined above; that is, it is a series of sentences in which the causal connections between the events mentioned are explicit or clearly implicit, and into which the relevant possible general laws may readily be inserted. Any number of such laws are not merely possible but actually available, e.g., if the two leading teams in the National League have won and lost the same number of games at the end of the regular season, the rules require that they resolve the tie by playing against each other until one of them has won two games.

(2) All the facts as stated are verifiably true and all the causal inferences are valid, and therefore the whole narrative explanation is historically true and accurate in every respect.

(3) Nevertheless, at a number of crucial points it is hard to see how particular effects were strictly entailed by a combination of antecedent causes and general laws. What, for example, is the general law which with the precondition (three hits and one out, among four men at bat) entails the replacement of one pitcher by another? Even if one elaborated further on the boundary conditions—and that can be done—it is difficult to see how general laws can be invoked and a strict entailment made to work here.

(4) It is true that once the substitute Brooklyn pitcher, Ralph Branca, whose mere presence in the game seems not amenable to narrative explanation (see above), released the ball, and once the fifth New York batter, Bobby Thomson, began his swing of the bat, a combination of a few special cases (mainly ballistic) of the general laws of motion with the National League ground rules on home runs suffices strictly to entail that Thomson hit a home run. It is hard, however, to envision the combination of conditions and laws that would strictly entail a decisive precondition of that home run: to wit, that Thomson decided to swing at Branca's pitch in the first place.

(5) Even if these problems of the logic of narrative explanation can be resolved, the account as presented raises a number of difficulties and questions. (*a*) Why does the explanation begin

with the play-off at the end of the regular season? On the face of it, in a regular season that ends in a tie, every game played throughout the season by the tied teams is of equal causal importance and therefore should receive equal treatment. (b) By the same token, why is a fuller account (inning-by-inning score) given of the last game of the official season than of the two previous games, and a still fuller account of the last half of the last inning of the last game?

(6) Most important, the explanation is historiographically pitiful, and the historian who offered it would immediately lose the historian's moral equivalent of a union card.

Given the problem with which we started, these difficulties go to the heart of the trouble. They make it clear that offering an answer in the form of a narrative explanation which is structurally determined solely by the logic of causal ascription is not an appropriate response to the difficulties or an adequate solution to the problem. Within the bounds of the logic of causal ascription there is no solution for them. That logic cannot justify the shifts in the scale of the story. Yet it is reasonable to suspect that one of the few things which most readers would intuitively regard as appropriate about the above dreary but true narrative response to the question about New York being in the World Series in 1951 would be precisely the successive expansions of the scale of the story. The reason for this is that the appropriate response to the question is not a true narrative explanation determined by the logic of causal ascription but the historical story truest to the past, determined by the rules of historical evidence and the rhetorical rules of historical storytelling. Of this larger context a true narrative explanation is a part, but only a part. If this is so, then the true historical story rightly determined by the rules of historical rhetoric will be preferable to a true narrative explanation because it communicates more knowledge and truth about the past than such an explanation does. But if that is so, then the rhetoric of history writing, not its logic alone, is implicated in providing increments of knowledge and truth about the past.

Let us continue with the example under examination, keeping in mind the problems of where to start the historical story and on what scale to tell it. Figure 1 describes the relative positions of the two contenders in the National League pennant race of 1951.

The first things to note in Figure 1 are the shifts in scale and the considerations which determined them. The overall consideration is that of telling a historical story in such a way as to maximize the increment of knowledge and truth communicated. That within a framework identical with the one in which the figure is constructed (the 154-game baseball season) it may be desirable to have no change of scale and not to tell a story at all becomes clear on considering the description of the American League season of 1939 in Figure 2.

Figure 2 is constructed on uniform scales for each axis, plotting the games won by the New York Yankees against the games won by the team in the league that was in second place. That this season calls for no narrative explanation is manifested by the nonconvergence of the lines in Figure 2, which shows (1) that by June 1, the Yankees were seven games ahead, (2) that thereafter

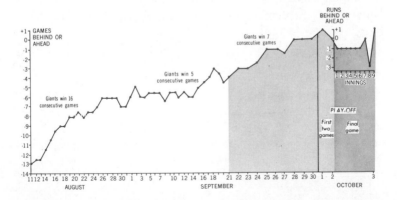

FIGURE 1. *The positions of the New York Giants in relation to the Brooklyn Dodgers in the 1951 pennant race, with standings shown at end of play on given date.*

the minimum gap between them and their nearest rival was six games, (3) that by the end of the season the Yankees led by seventeen games. In short, for more than the latter two-thirds of the season there was never a moment when it even looked like a pennant race, so that on the face of the record, to answer the question "How did the Yankees come to be in the World Series?" with a historical story would be a historiographic error: the even-paced, dull, and trivial chronicle which the effort would yield would itself demonstrate the inappropriateness of such a rhetorical response.

By the same token, the climbing line in Figure 1 indicates that the record of the 1951 National League season calls for a historical story, and that to write about its history without telling such a story is to fail to make the appropriate historiographic response. The data in Figure 1 start at the point where the extended historical story should begin: August 11, 1951, at the end of play. At that point New York was at its maximum distance behind Brooklyn, thirteen games; and the next day New York began a series of sixteen consecutive wins. For the next extension of the narrative and for the expansion of the scale of the graph, the directive of the record is more ambivalent. The options lie between (1) September 14, when, still six games behind, New

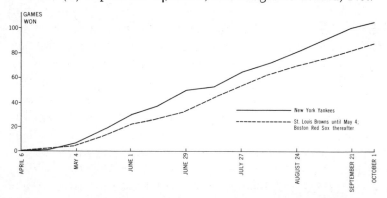

FIGURE 2. *The positions of the New York Yankees and the second-place American League team in the 1939 baseball season.*

York began a series of five consecutive wins which by September 18 moved it to within three games of Brooklyn and (2) September 21, when, four games behind, New York won the last seven games of the regular season. It had moved into a tie at the end of play September 28, kept the tie by winning the last two games of the regular season, and was again tied at the end of the second game of the play-off. It is to be noted that (1) although there are two options for starting this expansion, there are *only* two serious options, and (2) they have an identical *terminus ad quem*, the point at which the next expansion of scale begins in the final game of the play-off. Either of the above alternative solutions is historiographically correct; *any other* is incorrect. There may be two or more right answers to some historiographic, as to some mathematical, problems. This does not imply or entail that there are no wrong answers. This simple observation and distinction, evident to any mathematics student who has gotten as far as quadratic equations, seems to have escaped most historians.

The expansions of scale, then, are not arbitrary; each can clearly be justified from the historical record on historiographic grounds, and each expansion coincides with a period in telling about which the historical storyteller would extend the dimensions of his story. Three further points must be made.

(1) On the basis of true narrative explanation determined by the logic of causal connection, it proved impossible to determine where to begin the historical story of the 1951 pennant race or what dimensions to give to any of its parts. Indeed, since causal connection is subject both to infinite regress and to infinite ramification, and since that historical story and any other must have a beginning and finite dimensions of its parts, it is in principle impossible on the basis of the logic of narrative explanation alone to tell a historical story at all. On the other hand, the rhetoric of historical storytelling provided us with the means of recognizing whether there was a historical story to tell, where the story should start, and roughly what the relative dimensions of its parts should be. If this is so, (*a*) in the telling of a historical story, increments

of historical knowledge and truth are unattainable on the basis of the logic of narrative explanation alone, for on that basis alone it is impossible so much as to begin such a story; and (*b*) for achieving such increments, insights into the rhetoric of historical storytelling, whether experiential and implicit or discursive and explicit, are indispensable.

(2) The clock and the calendar provide no guidance to the appropriate dimensions of a historical story. Between those dimensions and mere duration, measured in homogeneous scaled increments, there is no congruence. The historical storyteller's time is not clock-and-calendar time; it is historical tempo. The problems involved in reasonably accurate determination of historical tempo have never been systematically studied, although results of the disaster of not studying them strew the historiographic landscape. But two points are clear. (*a*) Disproportions in historical stories induced by failure correctly to appraise historical tempo result in the telling of distorted stories about the past. To that extent they diminish, and correct perception of tempo increases, available knowledge of the past. (*b*) The logic of narrative explanation has nothing to say on the subject of historical tempo; it is a question that can be dealt with only in the area of the rhetoric of historical storytelling. And so once again the communication of increments of knowledge and truth about the past hinges on the correct solution of problems of historiography. (*c*) Correct determinations of historical tempo and the appropriate correlative expansions and contractions of scale in a historical story depend on the examination *in retrospect* of the historical record. That is to say, when the historian tells a historical story, he must not only know something of the outcomes of the events that concern him; he must use what he knows in telling his story.

In the case of writers of history, Gallie's interesting analogy between historical understanding and following a game or story breaks down, because it applies to the consumers of history, the readers, not to its producers, the writers.[2] The readers need not know the outcome of the story; and it is well if, at least, they do not know the writer's construal of the outcome, since not knowing it whets their curiosity and intensifies their engagement and vicarious participation in the story, thus augmenting their knowledge of the past. But unless the writer has the outcome in mind as he writes the story, he will not know how to adapt the proportions of his story to the actual historical tempo, since that is knowable only to one who knows the outcome. For example, the decisive point for transforming the proportions of the historical story of the 1951 pennant race was entirely unobserved, unpredictable, and unpredicted by any contemporary observer. On August 11, at the point of maximum distance between Brooklyn and New York, no one foresaw or could have foreseen that New York was on the point of beginning a sixteen-game winning streak that transformed the baseball season into a pennant race in which New York was the ultimate victor. Indeed, the perspective of the historical storyteller throughout should be double—that of a contemporary observer and that of one who knows about Bobby Thomson's home run; but it is from the latter perspective, not the former, that the historian can perceive the historical tempo and thus determine the appropriate proportion of the historical story.

HISTORICAL ANALYSIS / Telling a historical story is not the only way in which a writer of history can increase knowledge of the past, as we have seen in the case of the American League season of 1939. Even to the question "How did it happen that . . . ?" it is not always an appropriate response. Yet in the case in point, the response must have a historical character. The structure of Figure 2 suggests that it should take the form of historical analysis; for with its nonconverging lines it indicates that New York was a team so much better than any other in the league that it was beyond effective challenge. Consequently, to increase historical understanding there is nothing to do but analyze that betterness of New York, to seek out its ingredients and render them intelligible to the reader. Here, of course, the abundant surviving statistics of baseball provide a useful historical record to start with—the base-on-balls, strike-out, and earned-run averages of the pitchers; the batting and total base averages, the stolen bases, runs scored, and home runs of the hitters. (Fielding statistics, however, do not provide a satisfactory statistical basis for evaluating defensive performance in baseball.)

If the rhetoric of historical storytelling has received little attention from historians or others, the rhetoric of historical analysis has received none. When considering historical storytelling, the rhetoric of the fictive story offers a useful model; when considering historical analysis, the rhetoric of sciences in which the subject matter is less compatible with universal generalization than in physics might be appropriate. The almost complete lack of any serious concern with the problem may be due to the notion that the sciences have no rhetoric; but if one conceives of rhetoric as the organization of language appropriate to that particular kind of communication which is relevant to a particular activity, then any activity which is committed to verbal communication of its results has a rhetoric.

In recent years, instead of giving serious consideration to the serious problems of historical rhetoric, historians have engaged in considerable, and sometimes somewhat rancorous, discussion of the nonproblem of the relative merits of analysis and narrative in history writing. The discussion is footless because of two false assumptions: (1) that regardless of the character of the historical record, the historian has a wholly free option between analysis and narrative; (2) that these two historiographic modes mutually exclude each other, so that historians in all their work must opt wholly for the one or wholly for the other. With respect to the first assumption, we have seen in the instance of the two baseball seasons that the historical record presents us with constellations of events in which there is no serious option, where in one case to choose analysis, in the other to choose narrative, as the *predominant mode* would be a historiographic error and would prevent the historian from communicating what he knows about the past, and even from knowing it adequately.

In the second place, these modes are not mutually exclusive, and this again is evident with respect to our two "models." Although the mode of writing the history of the 1939 season should be predominantly analytical, still the force of the analysis would be strengthened by the resort to exemplary stories; and this is particularly the case with respect to fielding, in which the New York Yankees indeed excelled but which, because of limitations in the statistical record, lends itself better to anecdotal treatment, that is, to telling short illustrative stories. The case for the use of any analysis at all in the instance of the 1951 season might seem more dubious. The very fact of the tie at the end of the regular season could be taken as fair proof from a large sample of 154

TABLE 1. *Percentage of games won by the New York Giants and the Brooklyn Dodgers in the 1951 baseball season.*

	New York Giants	Brooklyn Dodgers
Beginning of season to August 11*	54%	66%
August 12 to end of season	84%	60%
Total season (154 games)	62%	62%

* As of August 11 the Giants had played 110 games and the Dodgers 106.

games that overall the two teams were so well matched as to make analysis an exercise in futility. Actually, an examination of the record yields a quite different result.

Table 1 shows the percentage of games won out of games played by each team up to August 11, and from August 12 to the end of the regular season. It clearly poses two analytical questions: (*a*) how to account for the marked superiority of Brooklyn in the first hundred-odd games of the season; (*b*) how to explain the overwhelming superiority of New York in the last forty-odd games. For such an undertaking, as we have seen, analysis is the proper historiographic mode. Note that the selection of analysis as the dominant mode for the first seven-tenths of the season does away with the need for telling an inevitably thin story and thus enables the historian to maintain the proportion called for by the demand of historical tempo. One further complication: The analysis would fail to reveal a part of what made the difference, the part, told by Eddie Stanky more than a decade later, about a battered battalion with pulled muscles, bad throwing arms, and cracked bones that still could not lose for winning. And thus, to do the analysis itself justice, the historian would have to afforce it with historical stories about Alvin Dark, Wes Westrum, Sal Maglie, and Stanky's own slides-into-bases that were hard to distinguish from overt assault and battery. Our two examples were themselves carefully selected extreme cases of records that call respectively for analysis and storytelling. In most history writing, the need for a mix of the historiographic modes of storytelling and analysis is even more obvious. The serious historiographic problem is not how to avoid the mix in order to maintain the superiority of one mode over the other, but how to proportion it and how to manage it.

In the foregoing "model" of the pennant race of 1951, the discussion has slipped—the author has intentionally allowed it to slip—insensibly from the problem of narrative explanation to the problems of historical storytelling. In this it has followed the curve, as it were, of historical curiosity itself, both in the reader and in the writer of history. The original question, "How did it come about that . . . ? ," has become the more amorphous "Tell me (or let me find out) more about. . . ." The demand is no longer merely for further *explanation*. A reasonably full explanation is presumably already in hand. That explanation itself has led reader and writer of history alike to shift the ground of their interest. Because of it they have become aware that they have stumbled onto one of the great events in baseball history, the event that culminated in Bobby Thomson's home run—the equivalent (in its sphere) of the defeat of the Armada, the battle of Stalingrad, the Normandy landings. What they want under these circumstances is not more or fuller explanation; what they want is confrontation with the riches of the event itself, a sense of vicarious participation in a great happening, the satisfaction of understanding what those great moments were like for the ordinarily cool Russ Hodges, Giant radio announcer, who, as the ball arched from Thomson's bat into the stands, went berserk and screamed into the microphone, "The Giants win the pennant! *The Giants win the pennant!* THE GIANTS WIN THE PENNANT!" And what those moments were like for those who saw what he saw and for those who heard him. Confrontation and vicarious participation are not historical explanation or explanation of any sort in any ordinary sense of the word. Yet clearly they are sometimes a part, and an indispensable part, of understanding the past as it actually was. Therefore, to argue that they have no place in historiography is at once arbitrary and absurd.

Finally, when the historian needs to bring those who seek to understand the past into confrontation with and vicarious participation in some part of it, he often finds the rhetoric of the sciences wholly inadequate for his purposes. In this sector of historiography it is hard to imagine a response to the proper demand on historians to render an accurate and effective account of the past that would be less appropriate than one couched in scientific rhetoric. In this sector, indeed, to do his work properly, *to tell the truth about the past,* the historian must marshal resources of rhetoric utterly alien to the rhetoric of the sciences in order to render his account forceful, vivid, and lively; to impart to it the emotional and intellectual impact that will render it maximally accessible and maximally intelligible to those who read it.

The analysis of historiography

The attitude of the historical profession to the writing of history has been ambivalent. Compared with the systematic attention historians have given to the techniques of historical investigation, their attention to the problems of historiography has been casual, and in their public judgments of the work of other historians they have tended to regard the rhetoric of history as at best a peripheral concern. On the other hand, some very able historians take far greater pains with their writing than would be warranted if the rhetoric of history were a mere pleasing embellishment not substantially involved in the advancement of the understanding of the past; and the consensus of the profession has ratified their practice by conferring on the most skillful writers of history rewards in prestige and pay that would be exorbitant if the yield of that skill were judged to be merely an amusing but supererogatory display of verbal pyrotechnics.

If the preceding arguments about the inseparability of the communication, and therefore the advancement, of historical knowledge from the rhetoric of history have any merit, then it would seem that a concerted effort to develop useful methods of analyzing historical rhetoric should stand high on the agenda of historians. In fact, however, their general concerns seem to be directed mainly toward two other areas, indeed, toward two nonproblems: (1) generalization and (2) the application of new knowledge in the social sciences to the study of history. The first is a nonproblem because in fact historians generalize and have generalized fruitfully at many levels for at least a couple of centuries, so that to raise at this late date the question of whether they do so or whether they ought to do so seems a little useless. Second, the application to the historical enterprise of any viable new technique for knowing is always desirable and is conditional only on the mastery of the technique and the identification of historical problems to which it can be usefully applied. In this respect the social sciences do not constitute a special case distinct from other techniques. Some historians have found some of the work of the social sciences useful for their particular purposes; others have not; still others have been preoccupied with other legitimate professional concerns. Their resistance to the demand for immediate and universal application to history of quantitative methods and of psychoanalytic insight does not seem to warrant the concern that it elicits from those who regard it as a chronic and possibly fatal disease of the historical profession as a whole. It does not appear to stand much above the level that reasonable professional prudence, sensible and limited skepticism, and resentment of new encroachments on limited resources of time, energy, and ability ordinarily generate.

Indifference to the problems of analyzing historiography, however, is easy to understand. In the first place, such analysis may well turn out to be a sterile exercise. In the second place, the need for analysis is evident only if one accepts the view that such attributes of historiography as accessibility, force, vividness, and depth are not merely decorative but have true noetic value. Although in unself-conscious practice many historians in fact accept this view, it remains submerged because of the counterthrust of an equally unself-conscious and incoherent assent to the ascription of noetic value only to the rhetoric of the sciences, especially to its denotative vocabulary and to its attributes of precision, simplicity, univocality, and so on.

In order to justify presenting the sketchy program for the analysis of historiography which this section will offer, it may be well to indicate the noetic bearing of at least one of the potential and requisite traits of historiography mentioned above—accessibility. In *On the Origin of Species* Charles Darwin says, "Nothing is easier to admit in words than the truths of the universal struggle for life, or more difficult—at least I have found it so—than constantly *to bear this conclusion in mind.*" The rhetorical problem that Darwin here points to is that of accessibility. It is a persistent problem for explanation in the narrative mode. The writer of history needs to be always watchful to see that pertinent previous generalizations, pertinent patterns of action previously identified, and pertinent parts of the story, already told, come to bear for the reader at the places where they are enlightening and revelatory. Even where it is technically accurate, dull history is bad history to the extent to which it is dull. By subjecting all the historian knows to the homogenizing and flattening operations of his own mechanical rhetoric, dull history blurs his findings for himself and for those who read his writing. Those findings then fail to become, or rapidly cease to be part of, the "workable reserve," the readily accessible knowledge, of the writer and reader, which remains concurrently present in their minds as the one composes and the other tries to follow the narrative or analysis. Consequently, in the course of events neither will see a partly ordered and patterned, and therefore partly intelligible, procession of change but a disjointed and arbitrary and therefore unintelligible one—just one damn thing after the other. A reader to whom almost nothing is communicated may reasonably suspect that the writer had almost nothing to communicate; but, as we have seen, because of the gap between knowing and communicating in history, this is not necessarily so. Rather, unintelligible communication is not communication at all; uncommunicated knowing can add no increment to the available body of knowledge, and frequently the failure to produce such an increment is a failure in historiography, the absence of accessibility.

Accessibility has been treated here as an absolute trait of history writing, and of course it is not so. It is relative not only to the historian's rhetorical capacities but also to the absorptive capacities of the historian's audience, which depend on their prior knowledge. An amount of detail necessary to render what he wishes to communicate accessible to one audience would simply clutter the text for another audience and stultify their imaginations, thus diminishing for that second audience the range of conceptions that the historian wants them to have in mind. The problem that this situation poses for the writer of history is a complex one; it is another of the many places where the rhetoric of the historian intersects and is entwined with the knowledge he communicates and the truth-value of what he has to say. There is not space to treat the matter of accessibility further here, but what is said below on the matter of word lists indicates some of the ramifications of the problem.

The analysis of historiography can conveniently be divided into macroanalysis, microanalysis, and analysis of structure. Macroanalysis is the analysis of an individual piece of history writing as a whole; microanalysis is the analysis of any fragment of historical rhetoric without primary regard to and out of relation to the historiographic whole of which it is a part. Analysis of structure deals with historiographic traits, devices, and practices which are common to all or to a very considerable number of historical works. Hitherto we have keyed our discussion of historiography to the rhetoric of scientific statement and explanation in order to make and keep clear the likenesses and differences between the two. We have suggested, however, that in at least one trait which it requires in order to communicate some of the things the historian knows—its reliance on a connotative and evocative vocabulary—the rhetoric of history is nearer to that of the fictive arts than to that of the natural sciences. So before examining the types of historiographic analysis, it will be appropriate to point out a major difference between historical and fictive rhetoric— the overriding commitment of historians to fidelity to the surviving records of the past.

FIDELITY TO RECORDS / The difference between historical and fictive rhetoric blurs slightly at the extreme limits, where, on the one hand, a novelist tells a story which he intends to reflect his conception of historical actualities and, on the other, a historian makes a story of a "typical case" that he imaginatively constructs out of his long experience with the historical record. The blurring itself becomes visible in a comparison of Conrad's *Nostromo* and Oscar Handlin's *The Uprooted,* but so does the difference that is blurred. For the worth of *Nostromo* as a novel would not diminish if the patterns of life Conrad ascribes to Costaguana, the imaginary Latin American republic which provides its setting and the substrate of its characters, were shown to be quite remote from extrinsic actuality. On the other hand, unless the record suggested that the immigrants' emotional response to their move to America was something like what *The Uprooted* imputes to them, the historiographic worth of *The Uprooted* would be nil, regardless of any merits that literary critics might ascribe to Handlin's prose style.

The standard of judgment of a fictive work does not depend on its compatibility with external actuality. The work as such depends for its authenticity or validity only on its relevance to the sector of general human experience which its author intends it to explore, describe, and render accessible. It can be true or false only to itself; and the knowledge which it communicates is independent of any particular in the record of man's past (though not, of course, independent of human experience in general). Or as A. J. Liebling put it, in treating the problems of a newspaperman, "To transmit more than half of what you understand is a hard trick, far beyond the task of the so-called creative artist who if he finds a character in his story awkward can simply change its characteristics. (Even to sex, *vide* Proust and Albertine. Let him try it with General de Gaulle.)"

It is precisely with Charles de Gaulle and his sort that reporters like Liebling and historians often have to deal. The standard of judgment of a historical work is ultimately extrinsic. Its authenticity, validity, and truth depend on the effectiveness with which it communicates knowledge (not misunderstanding) of the actual past congruent with the surviving record. The quality of its rhetoric is to be measured solely by its success in communicating such knowledge.

MACROANALYSIS / It follows from what has just been said that the unit of macroanalysis in historiography differs from the unit of macroanalysis in fictive studies. In the latter it is the entire particular work—novel or drama, ode or sonnet—considered as a self-contained unit. The macroanalyst can therefore demand of himself an examination of the whole relevant documentation and can reasonably expect those for whom he is writing to have the core element of that documentation (the work under analysis) before them. Ordinarily the macroanalyst of historiography cannot demand so much of himself, still less expect so much of his readers. For him the relevant documentation is the work itself plus the historical record of the episodes with which the author concerned himself, not merely the part he used but any important part that through errors of omission he failed to use. It is improbable that in most instances the analyst will command the full range of documentation; it is practically impossible under ordinary circumstances to expect the reader of the analysis to have the documentation in front of him.

Despite these limitations, some experiments in detailed macroanalysis seem desirable because only in such analysis does one deal with the actual unit of historiography—the historical work. Whether that work be a long treatise or a short article, its presentation is the means by which by far the largest part of the increments of historical knowledge is communicated. It is also the place where historians meet their worst failures—from the novices who, having researched their subject, have not a notion how to organize it for effective communication to those senior historians who have so completely surrendered to their own ineptitude as to transform verbosity into a criterion of excellence. By selecting a relatively short piece of historical writing based on a record of manageable dimension and reproducing both the piece and the record, it would be possible to perform the sort of detailed macroanalysis in historiography that is a commonplace in the field of literary criticism.[3]

Until a few such analyses are attempted, it is impossible to estimate what gains, if any, in the understanding of historiography may accrue from them; but it is hard to see why the macroanalysis of a historical study would be less fruitful of knowledge than the analysis of, say, *Waiting for Godot*. It is evident that unless such analysis is attempted, some aspects of the writing of history are bound to remain wrapped in mystery. For example, the present writer is a reasonably competent practitioner of history writing, and he has done a reasonable amount. One of the most effective sentences he has ever written in a historical essay is the following: "It was just the right thing for him to do." To understand why that simple declaratory statement composed of flat monosyllables should be effective would depend on a careful macroanalysis of the entire essay of which it is the last sentence.[4]

To the best of the writer's knowledge, up to the present no macroanalysis of any historical work has even been attempted on the scale and in the way above proposed. Only after it has been attempted several times will any estimate of its value be more than an idle guess. In the meantime, the discussion of historical story writing and historical analysis in previous sections of this article points to a very few of the problems—proportion of the story, historical tempo, balance of analysis and narrative—with which macroanalysis would have to concern itself.

MICROANALYSIS / Although microanalysis is primarily concerned with single small items of historical rhetoric, the radical severance of it from macroanalysis is not practically possible. Some sense of the whole framework remains essential, because only through that sense can one arrive at a judgment on the ultimate efficacy and appropriateness of a given small item of historical writing which is a part of a historiographic whole. "The Army of the Covenant of the Scots with their God marched across the Tweed to rescue their sore beset English brethren" is historiographically sound, if its general context requires at the point of its introduction a quick communication of the spirit in which the Scots took the field in 1644. If the total context is the logistical problems created by the presence of a considerable military force in the agriculturally unproductive north of England in the mid-seventeenth century, however, a less allusive statement, detailing the number of Scots who entered the northern counties and their daily requirement of food and forage, would be rather more appropriate.

For the examination of any single element of historical rhetoric, macroanalysis (although not necessarily on the scale above suggested) is desirable. Only by means of it can one finally judge whether that element is appropriate, for its appropriateness is a function of the *whole* context of which it is a part. Ostensible grotesquerie—Alexander in full plate armor—may be appropriate enough if we see the whole picture, as Panofsky showed in discussing medieval representations of that hero. Because, however, the single historical statement has a dual context—both the work of history in which it is embedded and the actuality of the past to which it refers—it is possible to clarify some of the specific characteristics of the rhetoric of history by microanalysis considered with minimal reference to the total structure of the historical work of which the fragment under microanalysis is a part. In effect, given a five-page account of the battle of Waterloo embedded in a historical work, by referring the account to the historical record, it is usually possible to say within the limits the historian set for the account whether it is historiographically sound at the level of microanalysis. On examining it in connection with the whole work, however, we might alter our judgment on the grounds that in its macroanalytic context it is disproportionately long or short, that it is dissonant with the rest of the book, or even that it is wholly irrelevant.

Microanalysis of historiography is therefore provisional in the judgments it yields on the material it deals with, but it does at least yield provisional judgments. Here we have space to treat only one hypothetical example of microanalysis. Let us suppose a historian faced with the problem of dealing in two pages with the character and administration of U.S. President Warren G. Harding. One can conceive of his choosing to do it in the style of the late Ring Lardner and with a rhetoric—a vocabulary and syntax—as close to Lardner's as his own sense of historiographic proprieties and that of his editor would permit. Or one can conceive of a characterization the whole tone of which was heavily heroic in vocabulary and syntax—so long as the undertone made it evident that the verbal heroics were mock heroics. What would be wholly inappropriate to a brief characterization of Harding and his entourage would be a rhetoric of intentional, unrelenting, and unremitting solemnity. On the other hand, briefly to characterize Abraham Lincoln in either of the former rhetorical modes would not only be bad taste, it would be bad historiography; and the historian who employed either would promptly be marked by his peers as inept and incompetent. For Lincoln was a serious man (which did not prevent him from being a very humorous one) and a serious historical figure, and any attempt to present him in a short sketch which failed to reflect this fact would to that extent fail to communicate to the reader something he needed to understand about the realities of a part of the past. It would thereby not only fail to advance but perhaps would even diminish his knowledge and understanding of the past, his grasp of part of its meaning, his store of historical truth.

The implications of this excursus on the use of microanalysis of historiography in connection with characterizing actual persons of the past are worth a little further attention, since one of the persistent problems of history writing, calling for microanalysis, is that of characterization. In effect, in many kinds of historical investigation the historian encounters persons in the record of the past. He can disregard them as persons and transform them into, say, numbers; and a demographic historian quite rightly does just this, simply because that is in fact the aspect under which he encounters them. He is like a man trying to get on a full elevator who encounters the persons already aboard merely as "a full elevator." But that is not always, or even often, the way a historian encounters persons in the record of the past. If he encounters them *as persons*, an attempt to avoid characterizing those implicated in an important way in the account he is rendering is a refusal to deal faithfully with the record of the past.

No one whose judgment is worth serious consideration has ever suggested that historians must never characterize people they encounter in the past; and it is at least arguable that the normal rhetoric of history is such that a historian dealing with extensive data on the deeds and words of a person of the past cannot avoid characterizing him, that the only question is whether he characterizes him well or ill, whether he does him justice or

The Rhetoric of History

injustice. Nor has anyone ever argued that it is desirable or indeed even possible adequately to characterize a man in the wholly denotative rhetoric that is appropriate to scientific discourse. Indeed, the very phrase "do justice," which is quite appropriate to describe the goal of characterizing a man, is itself so massively connotative, so indispensably imprecise, as to render nugatory any hope of accomplishing with a sterilized denotative vocabulary and syntax a mission so vaguely described and imprecisely delimited. And yet it is possible by microanalysis of historical writing to arrive at judgments not merely of "bad" and "good" but also of "false" and "true" (or at least "truer") with respect to the connotative rhetoric which a historian chooses to employ in fulfilling his commitment to do justice to the character of a man. Nor is there any great mystery about this in the case of men concerning whom the historical record is reasonably ample. Considering the rhetorical possibilities as a very broad spectrum and also as a complete spectrum within the bounds of the rhetorical potentialities of the common language structure, there will be areas of that spectrum into which what is known about a particular man cannot be fit without manifest distortion of the record and areas into which it fairly fits, although in both cases there may be several such areas. This was manifestly the case in the instances of Harding and Lincoln dealt with above. But to distort the record is precisely to communicate ignorance rather than knowledge, misunderstanding rather than understanding, falsehood rather than truth.

The only necessary qualification here is that no historian does, and no sensible historian claims to, communicate the whole truth about a man, since there are many things about any man living or dead which no human being, not even the man himself, knows. The full knowledge on which alone a final judgment is possible exists only in the mind of God. The facts remain that in certain reaches of historiography the characterization of men is inescapable, that the rhetoric of such characterization is inescapably nonscientific, and that the knowledge, understanding, and truth communicated by the history of which the characterization is a part will in some measure depend on how well or ill the historian deploys the resources of this inevitably nonscientific rhetoric, on the appropriateness of his response to the demands that the historical record makes on his ability to use nonscientific language in delineating a character. The curious problems that this situation implies deserve further examination.

ANALYSIS OF STRUCTURE / The general analysis of historiography deals with those traits and devices of historical rhetoric which are unique to the writing of history, or, more frequently, with those traits and devices which historians use in a unique way, a way which differentiates them from their use in the sciences or in the fictive arts. In the following treatment of the general analysis of historiography we will focus attention on three devices of the rhetoric of history: (1) the footnote, (2) the quotation in the text, (3) the word list; and we will concentrate on what differentiates the historian's use of these devices from the use scientists make of their homologues in scientific rhetoric.

Footnotes / Historians and scientists both use footnotes, and for one purpose they use them in about the same way: they use them to cite to the "literature" of the subject or problem about which they are writing. Historians, however, also use footnotes in a variety of other ways. One way historians use them and physicists do not is to cite to the historical record, the substrate of evidence on which historians erect their accounts of the past. Citation to that record is the way a historian makes his professional commitment clear in action, as the report on the experiment is the way a physicist makes his commitment clear. In both instances it is a commitment to maximum verisimilitude (which does not mean exact replication in every detail). For the physicist it is maximum verisimilitude to the operations of nature as glimpsed through consideration of the experimental cluster; for the historian, verisimilitude to the happenings of the past as glimpsed through consideration of the surviving record.

The well-nigh universal use of footnotes to the record by historians indicates that they are all still committed to writing about the past, as Ranke put it, *wie es eigentlich gewesen,* as it actually happened. In today's somewhat more sophisticated language, we might say that historians are concerned and committed to offer the best and most likely account of the past that can be sustained by the relevant extrinsic evidence. Let us call this statement about the historian's commitment the "reality" rule.

Historians employ the footnote for a host of residual matters other than citations to the record—lists of names, minor qualifications of assertions made in the text, polemic criticisms of other historians, short statistical tables, suggestions for future historical investigation, and many more. This raises two questions. (1) Amid the apparent chaos of "residual" footnotes, are there any rules at all regulating their use? (2) What is the relation of any rules found to the "reality" rule?

As to the first question, the application of any rule about footnotes requires an act of judgment in each case, and among historians judgment about the uses of residual footnotes differs. It might seem that in matters of judgment, as in those of taste, there is no disputing. But is this so? Let us consider an example.

At Shilbottle, in the case of three separate parcels of meadow, 31, 20 and 14 acres respectively, the first rendered 42s. in 1415–16 and 30s. in 1435–6, the second 28s. in 1420–1 and 23s. in 1435–6, and the third 24s. in 1422–3 and 14s. in 1435–6. At Guyzance 6½ husbandlands each rendered 13s.4d. in 1406–7, but 10s. in 1435–6.

At Chatton and Rennington, on the other hand, the situation was more stable. At Rennington the clear revenues were £17.8s.3d. in 1435–6 and £17 in 1471–2 and at Chatton £40.18s.7d. in 1434–5 and £36.18s.7d in 1472–3. At Chatton the decline was due to a fall in the value of the farm of the park, from £6.13s.4d. to £2.13s.4d. . . .

The above passage is embedded in the *text* of a study of the wealth of a magnate family in the fifteenth and early sixteenth centuries and the effect on that wealth of concurrent changes in the economy, the military apparatus, and the political situation in England. Can anyone suggest that embedding it in the text instead of quarantining it in a footnote was *not* an error of judgment? But to say it was one is to imply a *rule* from which the erroneous judgment was a deviation. Can such a rule, a "law" of historical rhetoric or historiography, be stated? Approximately the rule might go: "Place in footnotes evidence and information which if inserted in the text diminish the impact on the reader of what you, as a historian, aim to convey to him."

So although in the matter of the use of residual footnotes judgment is inescapable, we are not at all confronted with mere arbitrariness but with a reasonably precise rule or law. We may name it the "maximum impact" rule. Inevitably, marginal situations exist in which historians disagree about how to achieve maximum impact or about the success of a certain rhetorical presentation. The existence of such marginal situations, however, does not mean that all situations are marginal and that therefore there is no rule, or that any rule is as good as any other. Lawyers have a saying that hard cases make bad law, but they do not feel impelled thereupon to argue that there are no easy cases and no good law. Because there are some matters both substantive and procedural concerning which they are very uncertain, some historians have fallen victim to the notion that everything about the past and about writing about it is infected with a total uncertainty. Yet this is clearly not so in the case of the residual footnote, where there was no difficulty in finding a rule not heavily infected with uncertainty.

What, then, is the relation of the two rules—the "reality" rule and "maximum impact" rule—to each other? In the example of data that, by the second rule, ought to be withdrawn from the text and consigned to a residual footnote, those data are informative and relevant with respect to the substantive historical argument the historian is presenting, and they are as complete, as explicit, and as exact as possible. But the historian is also committed to conveying to the reader with maximum impact his conception and understanding of the past as it actually happened, the "reality" of the first rule. And paradoxically, this implies that in the interest of conveying historical reality to the reader with maximum impact, the rules of historiography may require a historian to subordinate completeness, explicitness, and exactness to other considerations. If this is so, it indeed separates historiography from the rhetoric of the sciences as currently conceived.

Quotation in the text / Again, although both may quote in the text, there is a major difference here between the historians and the physicists. If physicists could not quote in the text, they would not feel that much was lost with respect to advancement of knowledge of the natural world. If historians could not quote, they would deem it a disastrous impediment to the communication of knowledge about the past. A luxury for physicists, quotation is a necessity for historians, indispensable to historiography.

The kind of quotation that historians deem indispensable is quotation from the record. Again two questions arise. (1) Is there any rule governing quotation from the record? (2) How does that rule relate to the "reality" rule?

Consider a hypothetical case of inept quotation. Suppose in writing the history of the Civil Rights Act of 1964, a historian were to quote verbatim from the *Congressional Record* the entire debate on the act in both the House and the Senate. The result would be relevant, exact, and accurate—and not only the judgment but the sanity of the historian would fall under serious question. Again the paradox: maximum completeness, accuracy, and exactness are not always essential or even desirable in the historian's work of trying to tell the reader what really happened. Now consider an adept quotation taken from E. Harris Harbison's *The Christian Scholar in the Age of the Reformation:*

> Erasmus had absorbed [Lorenzo] Valla's historical perspective, his sense of the historical discontinuity between pagan antiquity and the Christian era . . . a sensitivity to anachronism. On one occasion he ridiculed the absurdity of the practice . . . of using Ciceronian words to describe an utterly different modern world: *"Wherever I*

turn my eyes I see all things changed, I stand before another stage
and I behold a different play, nay, even a different world." The
world of Cicero (or of Paul) can be understood and even in a
sense relived—but only if we recognize that it had its unique
existence, once, in a past now dead.[5]

The function of Harbison's brief but apt quotation from
Erasmus is not mere validation or proof of his assertions; he could
as well have effected that by citation or quotation in a footnote.
By using Erasmus' own words in the text, he sought and won a
response not merely of assent but of conviction, not just "Yes,"
but "Yes, indeed!" Nothing Harbison could have said about
Erasmus' sense of history could produce the conviction about it
that Erasmus' own assertion of his intense feeling of distance
from antiquity produces.

The quotation aims at something in addition to conviction,
however. The quotation communicates the historian's own view
of what happened in the past by the particular means of confrontation. It says in effect, "In my judgment the most economical
way at this point to tell you what I believe Erasmus meant and to
convince you that he meant it is to confront you directly with
what Erasmus said." This provides us with a third general rule of
historiography—an "economy-of-quotation" rule: Quote from
the record of the past only when and to the extent that confrontation with that record is the best way to help the reader to an
understanding of the past *wie es eigentlich gewesen*. It is evident,
however, from the instance of the hypothetical case of the *Congressional Record* that mere confrontation with the *record* of the
past is not necessarily the best way to achieve this understanding
or even to achieve historical confrontation. Indeed, far from
being a clear glass window through which the reader may capture
an image of the past, quotation from the record injudiciously
used can be a thick opaque wall that cuts him off from it.
Granted that confrontation is an appropriate means for a historian to avail himself of in his efforts to convey to the reader an
understanding of what actually happened, it then becomes pos-

sible to transcend the paradox previously noted. It opens up the possibility that the microscopic means of historiography have to be adapted to its macroscopic ends and that it is part of the task of the writer of history to mediate understanding and confrontation by devices of the rhetoric of history less direct but more compelling, more to the purpose than a simple maximizing of completeness, accuracy, and exactness.

The word list / The word list is a device useful both in the rhetoric of history and in the rhetoric of the sciences. (It is a sequence of words, usually nouns, whose relations as members of a set are often made evident by a sequence of commas and/or semicolons, the conjunction "and," or typographical arrangement in a table.) Consider the following lists:

> An inert element will not react or enter into chemical combination with any other element. In order of increasing atomic weight the inert elements are helium (4), neon (20), argon (39), krypton (84), xenon (131), and radon (222).
>
> The average incomes of only three of the learned professions fall into the first quartile of all average incomes. In descending order of quartile and rank, the average incomes of members of the learned professions were as follows: surgeons (1,2), physicians (1,4), dentists (1,7), college professors (2,23), high school teachers (3,41), clergymen (3,47), grade school teachers (3,52).

The first list is scientific; the second, historiographic. They are in many respects similar. In intent the words composing them are wholly denotative. They are not supposed to cast any shadow, to connote or evoke anything. Their arrangement (ascending order, descending order) is dictated entirely by considerations of rational utility. They both implicitly relate to an informational framework equally denotative in intention—the periodic table of all chemical elements, the table of average incomes of the total population classified by profession and trade. Both listings aim to achieve a purpose universal in the rhetoric of the sciences, common but not universal in the rhetoric of history. The scientist always wants the state, process, and set of entities he is dealing with so labeled that the labels unambiguously and unequivocally point to that state, process, and set only. For the scientist's purpose when he is formally communicating what he knows, words need to be free of contamination, of connotation, evocation, and emotive force, as sterile as the apparatus in an operating room. Otherwise he may find the wires of communication snarled and, as a consequence, have to rectify avoidable confusion. In this matter the historian's purpose often coincides exactly with that of the scientist. It is only under the conditions and with a vocabulary of the kind above specified that he can to his own satisfaction transmit some of the kinds of information and understanding that he intends to communicate. Yet even the very close approximation to scientific rhetoric exemplified by the foregoing historiographic word list deviates from the scientific standard in ways that help to differentiate both the problems and the purposes of history from those of the sciences. Consider the question "Is not zinc (65) also an inert element?" To answer this question one can pour hydrochloric acid over zinc. Since one of the yields of this operation is zinc chloride ($ZnCl$), a chemical combination or compound, zinc is not an inert element.

The taxonomic system of chemical elements—the periodic table—is thus free of ambiguity. Suppose, on the other hand, the question were raised whether clergymen and elementary and high school teachers should be included as members of the learned professions when the executives of large corporations are excluded. The question points to doubts about a system of classification that might include store-front preachers and graduates of retrograde teacher-training colleges among members of the learned professions while excluding the products of the better graduate schools of business administration. These doubts thus revolve about the identifying traits of the learned professions and the expediencies involved in the selection of any one set as against alternative sets of traits for classificatory purposes.

In any developed natural science, expediency in the choice of traits for a taxonomic system depends on the "importance" of the traits within the bounds of that science—e.g., in chemistry, valence and atomic weight as against color and taste. And importance is graded by applicability within the framework of generalizations or "scientific laws" that articulate the structure of the science in question and form the basis of its dominant mode of explanation. The dominant mode of historical explanation, narrative, emits no such clear, uniform signal for determining importance, and therefore in historiography the expediencies of alternative taxonomic systems often remain equivocal and debatable. It is this situation which generates the interminable discussions among historians about whether sixteenth-century monarchies were *really* absolute, whether the Indians in the *encomiendas* in the Spanish colonies were *really* in servitude, whether the owner–operator of a small newsstand is *really* a capitalist. Such discussions seem futile because they purport to deal directly with the actual character of the past, a historical problem, when in fact they are concerned with the relative expediencies of alternative taxonomic devices for communicating knowledge of the past, a historiographic problem. The problem of taxonomy so considered, however, is anything but trivial (1) because classification systems both condition effectiveness of communication and channel the course of historical thinking, and (2) because in the very nature of the rhetoric of history, terms like "capitalist," "absolute," and "learned profession" cannot be rendered wholly denotative to the consumer of history writing. Given the nonscientific values pursued in historiography, a historian using such items will have to decide, for the purposes of the story or narrative explanation engaging him at the moment, how much time and effort he should expend in separating the connotative values from those terms and how important those connotative values are for advancing the historical understanding of the matter at hand. It is evident, in any case, that the general analysis of historical rhetoric involves a study of problems of taxonomy in history closer than any undertaken up to now.

One further trait of the above historiographic word list needs to be noted: it is either elliptical or meaningless. It acquires meaning only if time and place are specified, whereas no such specification is necessary in the above scientific list. A statement whose formal structure and manifest purpose seem very close to those that characterize the natural sciences illustrates the dominant time–place specificity of the rhetoric of history as against the dominant time–space generality of the rhetoric of the sciences. Thus the analysis of a historical word list reinforces the conclusion that has emerged time and again in the course of this discussion of the rhetoric of history: despite occasional likenesses, historiography is radically unassimilable to the rhetoric of the natural sciences.

This can be even more effectively illustrated by another example of the historiographic use of a list.

> The Christian Revival, that intensification of religious sentiment and concern that began long before 1517 and extended long beyond, in its full span had room for Cardinal Ximenes and Girolamo Savonarola; Martin Luther and Ignatius Loyola, the Reformed churches and the Jesuits, John of Leiden and Paul IV, Thomas Cranmer and Edmund Campion and Michael Servetus.

The names constitute a historiographic list, intended to serve a particular purpose of the rhetoric of history. It emits a signal, and what the signal says to all who hear it is: "Draw on the reservoir of your knowledge of the times in which these men lived to give meaning to this list." If that reservoir is altogether empty, then inevitably the list will itself be historiographically empty, meaningless, a mere collection of sounds, just as the sentences about the inert gases are empty of meaning to any who have no notion of what a chemical element or a chemical reaction or atomic weight is. The reason for this similarity is that in the present case both the historiographic rhetoric and the scientific rhetoric presuppose that the reader already possesses a body of precise and exact knowledge of the particular universes to which they refer. The scientific and the second historiographic statement both

conform to the "reality" rule; they are meaningless unless there
are such elements as helium, neon, and argon; and unless there
were such men as Loyola, Cranmer, and Paul IV. Yet the second historiographic list serves a rhetorical function quite different from that served by the scientific list. First, consider the
order of the two lists. Given the gases' common trait of inertness,
the order of the scientific list indicates the scientist's normal
preoccupation with establishing scalable differences of homogeneous traits—in this case, weight. In the historiographical list,
on the other hand, no such preoccupation is discernible, yet the
arrangement of the names lies at the very heart of the matter.

Note that there are three alternative ways of writing the
historiographic list, all of which maintain the essential arrangement, to convey whatever information it contains.

(1) Cardinal Ximenes and Girolamo Savonarola, Martin
Luther and Ignatius Loyola, the Reformed churches and the
Jesuits, John of Leiden and Paul IV, Thomas Cranmer and Ed-
mund Campion and Michael Servetus.

(2) The pre-Reformation cardinal who reformed the church
in Spain, and the pre-Reformation monk who was burned at the
stake for his reforming efforts in Florence; the first great figure
of the Reformation and the first great figure of the Counter Reformation; the cutting edge of the Protestant attack and the cutting
edge of the Catholic counterattack; the most fanatical prophet of
the radical Reformation and the most fanatical pope of the era of
religious strife; the Protestant martyred by the Catholics, the
Catholic martyred by the Protestants, and the martyr who escaped
death at the hands of the Catholics only to receive it at the hands
of the Protestants.

(3) Cardinal Ximenes, the pre-Reformation cardinal who
reformed the church in Spain, and Girolamo Savonarola, the pre-
Reformation monk who was burned at the stake for his reforming
efforts in Florence; Luther, the first great figure of the Reformation, and Loyola, the first great figure of the Counter Reformation; the Reformed churches, the cutting edge of the Protestant
attack, and the Jesuits, the cutting edge of the Catholic counterattack. . . .

The persons balanced in tension with one another are the same for all three versions of the list, and the arraying is identical in all three. On mathematical principles, a member of any of the lists should be freely substitutable for the corresponding member of either of the other two, but in writing history *this is not so*. Each list must retain its integrity. On what grounds can a historian choose among the three? One might argue that the second list is preferable to the first since it explicates the rationale upon which the persons in the first list were arrayed and that, in point of information about the past, the third is best of all, since it both names the persons and explicates the rationale of their array. Yet a reasonably experienced historian committed to communicating what he understands about the past actually chose the *first* option—the bare list of names with no indication as to his grounds for choosing them or for ordering them as he did. His choice is explicable when related to an earlier observation about the signal emanated by the list: "Draw on the reservoir of your knowledge of the times in which these men lived to give meaning to the list." The writer assumed that most of his readers could and would in fact draw from their particular reservoirs the items of general information in the second and third lists.

The effect of spelling out that information, however, is to emit another kind of rhetorical signal, a stop signal: "Stop drawing on the reservoir of your knowledge. I have already told you how I want you to think about these men." And this stop signal is just what the writer did *not* want the list to emit. The third version of the list is more exact, more overtly informative than the bare names in the first list, and just for that reason it is more empty, less ample. It dams up the informed reader's imagination instead of letting it flow freely, bringing with it the mass of connotation and association that those names have for him. Therefore, to prevent such a blockage the writer chose the first list. In doing so, he made a judgment. He judged (or gambled) that the connotative, evocative list would communicate a fuller meaning than the exact one, that it would more effectively confront the reader with the reality of the Christian revival, and that therefore it was the more appropriate device for advancing the reader's understanding of it. Whether he was correct in his judgment or not is immaterial. In setting forth his findings, a scientist never needs to make such a judgment at all. Scientific rhetoric is purposefully constructed to free him of that need by barring connotative terms and evocative devices. To a scientist the idea that he had to choose between a rhetoric of clarity and precision on the one hand and one of evocative force on the other would be shocking. The idea that the writer of history has to select between mutually exclusive ways of setting forth the same data and that the knowledge of history that he conveys depends in some measure on his judgment in selecting among alternative rhetorical devices is perhaps as disturbing and perplexing. But one is impelled to the latter conclusion by an investigation of the peculiarities of the way writers of history use footnotes, quotations, and word lists.

Codification of historiographic principles

The whole preceding article may be regarded as a prolegomenon to a codification of principles of historiography. Its aim has not been to produce such a codification but (1) to indicate that it might be possible to produce one and (2) to educe a few of the rules that would have place there. It has been concerned time and again to mark the irreducible differences that separate the rhetoric of history from that of natural sciences because, given the prestige of those sciences and the striking similarity of some of the objectives of history writing and science writing, there is a danger that an attempt to codify the principles of historiography might take the form of a systematic effort to reduce as far as possible those principles to the ones current in the natural sciences. This indeed has already been the outcome of attempts by analytic philosophers from Carl

Hempel to Morton White to codify the rules of historiography. The outcome of such an effort would be catastrophic, not because it would be an utter failure but because it would be a partial success. It would succeed in codifying rules about a great deal of what historians write in a way that would relate it closely to what scientists write. It might then be inferred that only the part of the rhetoric of history which can be articulated with that of the sciences is fit for communicating what in the course of their researches historians learn about the past, or that only that part is amenable to codification. In the foregoing discussion, however, we have already seen that in the writing of history it is often necessary to employ language in ways that scientists quite properly reject for communicating the results of their investigations. Therefore, instead of extending our knowledge of the past, to limit historiography to those statements about the past which can be formulated in the rhetoric of the sciences would sharply constrict it.

The rational procedure in attempting to elicit general rules of historiography would be, rather, to make a series of analyses of the kinds classified and discussed in the previous section, taking as their subject pieces of historical writing which on the basis of a broad consensus of historians have been extraordinarily successful in transmitting what their writers knew about the past. It is impossible of course, to predict in substance the outcome of such an analytical effort. Because in the section on general analysis we were able to elicit a few sample rules, it may, however, be possible to hazard a conjecture about its form. On the basis of that small sample one might conjecture that a codification of the rules of historiography would resemble a manual of military strategy more than a handbook of physics. It would consist of a number of maxims generally applicable to the solution of recurrent problems in writing history, leaving the identification of his particular problems and application of the maxims to the experience of the trained historian.

The most important professional use of such codification would be precisely in the training of historians. Historians do not lack the ability to discriminate between historiography which badly and inadequately communicates what a historian knows and historiography which communicates it well. Unfortunately, because that ability is now acquired almost wholly through experience rather than through a combination of experience and systematic knowledge, it is rarely and inefficiently transmitted from teacher to pupil. Indeed, the systematic training of historians is almost solely given over to the transmission of competence in the operations they must perform *before* they engage in the activity that defines their craft—the writing of history. Many historians receive the doctoral degree, which is supposed to certify their competence in their craft, without ever being compelled to rewrite anything they have written after having it subjected to rigorous and systematic criticism. The chronic ineptitude that hosts of historians display in their attempts to communicate what they know is a testimonial to the inadequacy of their training in this respect, or to its complete neglect. This ineptitude may suggest the desirability of an attempt to state coherently at least part of what the better historians know experientially about writing history and demonstrate visibly in the consistent appropriateness of their responses to the problems of historiographic statement.

Theoretical implications

The examination of historiography in this article has at various points suggested what becomes quite evident in the treatment of narrative explanation as against historical storytelling and in the section on the analysis of the form of a historical work—that the practices of historians in writing history may have some peculiar and serious implications in that wide area of human concern in which men struggle with the difficult problems of the meaning and nature of knowledge, understanding, and truth. The principal relevant points that have emerged may be summarized as follows.

First, historiography is a rule-bound discipline by means of which historians seek to communicate their knowledge of the past.

Second, the relation of writing history, of its rhetoric, to history itself is quite other than it has traditionally been conceived. Rhetoric is ordinarily deemed icing on the cake of history, but our investigation indicates that it is mixed right into the batter. It affects not merely the outward appearance of hisory, its delightfulness and seemliness, but its inward character, its essential function—its capacity to convey knowledge of the past as it actually was. And if this is indeed the case, historians must subject historiography, the process of writing history, to an investigation far broader and far more intense than any that they have hitherto conducted.

Third, there is an irreducible divergence between the rhetoric of history and the rhetoric of science; the vocabulary and syntax that constitute the appropriate response of the historian to his data are neither identical with nor identifiable with the vocabulary and syntax that constitute the appropriate response of the scientist to his data. But the historian's goal in his response to the data is to render the best account he can of the past as it really was. Therefore, by his resort to the rhetoric of history, regardless of its divergence from that of the sciences, the historian affirms in practice and action his belief that it is more adequate than the latter as a vehicle to convey the kind of knowledge, understanding, truth, and meaning that historians achieve. Indeed, instances were discovered in which, in order to transmit an increment of knowledge and meaning, the very rules of historiography demand a rhetoric which sacrifices generality, precision, control, and exactness to evocative force and scope—a choice entirely out of bounds according to the rules of scientific statement. And this implies that in the rhetoric of history itself there are embedded assumptions about the nature of knowing, understanding, meaning, and truth and about the means of augmenting them that are not completely congruent with the corresponding assumptions in the sciences, at least insofar as the philosophy of science has succeded in identifying them.

Historiography has generated a crisis in the currently dominant Anglo–American school of philosophy, the school that has as its main subgroups logical positivism, the philosophy of science, and language analysis. That it has done so is evident from a cursory examination of the index of one of the more recent works on history writing by an analytical philosopher, Arthur Danto.[6] Besides the philosophical magnates, living and dead, tangentially involved in the dialogue—Ayer, Bradley, Dewey, Hume, Kant, Lewis, Peirce, Ryle, Russell, Wittgenstein —the index mentions Agassi, Danto, Donagan, Dray, Gallie, Gardiner, Gellner, Hempel, Mandelbaum, Nagel, Passmore, Popper, Scriven, Walsh, and Watkins, all of whom since 1940 have directly confronted the problems that in their view historiography poses for philosophy; and the list is by no means complete. The close attention that this group of philosophers has directed to history writing is especially significant because of their central preoccupation with the way in which language communicates knowledge, understanding, meaning, and truth. In the broadest sense this large collective enterprise has been trying to define the relationship between the practices of writers of history and the nature of knowledge, understanding, meaning, and truth, especially as revealed in the structure of scientific rhetoric.

The preceding prolegomenon to an inquiry into the rules of the rhetoric of history provides a clue to the character of the crisis (symptomatically marked by the profusion of their output on the subject) with which the writing of history has confronted the analytical philosophers. History has posed for them a very difficult puzzle. Most historians in theory, *all* in practice, treat their subject as if through their current methods and their current rhetoric they were achieving and transmitting increments of knowledge about it. That is to say, they declare that if a piece of historical work is well done and properly set down, readers will

know more about the past after they have read it than they did
before. And for practical purposes very few people have seriously
doubted the propriety of this claim (the few that do, appear to
have read very little history). And yet historiography—the forms
of statement historians adopt, their rhetoric—does not seem to
fit into the sign structure suitable for scientific explanation, the
classical rhetoric for communicating increments of knowledge,
and most historians have been either indifferent or actively hos-
tile to the notion that in the interest of rendering an account of
the past as it actually was, they ought to elaborate and consistently employ such a sign structure. It is with this paradox that
so many analytical philosophers have tried to deal systematically
since 1940.

The course of this large collective effort is far too complex
and has had too many ramifications to be dealt with here in detail. Briefly, the initial supposition by Carl Hempel,[7] set forth
above, was (1) that the universal valid model of explanation is
that of the natural sciences, (2) that this consists in linking an
event to general laws in such a way that the event is entailed by
the laws through strict deduction, (3) that any activity of a historian that does not achieve this end does not explain anything,
(4) that although in some instances historians can perform the
necessary operations, they rarely do so, and therefore (5) that by
and large in most of their actual operations historians explain
nothing. Twenty-five years of intensive discussion by analytical
philosophers has taken off from, and resulted in a number of
proposals for modifying, this rigorist position. It seems likely
that the dis-ease which some of these modifications manifest is in
part the consequence of an often unarticulated sense on the part
of analytical philosophers who have read history books that the
actual procedures of historians, for knowing, understanding, and
giving an account of the past as it actually was, do achieve their
explicit or implicit purpose. In the course of bringing about a
partial confrontation of the general-law theory of explanation
with historiography, the analytical philosophers discovered a
number of facts about the latter which because of their apparent

deviation from the general-law or scientific model caused them perplexity. Among these were (1) that for many purposes of "explanation why," historians do not resort to general laws but to truisms; (2) that when historians are confronted with the question "Why?" their frequent, indeed normal, impulse is not to recite or seek relevant general laws, as a scientist would do, but to tell a story, and that such a story often seems to provide a satisfying answer to the question "Why?" while a general law does not; (3) that the questions historians are often most heavily engaged in answering are not why-questions at all but what-questions (and also, one might add parenthetically, who-, when-, and where-questions); and (4) that a great deal of the activity of historians can be construed as having explanation as its aim only by so far extending the meanings of explanation current in analytical philosophy as to destroy even the appearance of synonymy and to impose well-nigh unbearable strains even on analogy.

In the process of coping with these problems, the analytical philosophers have produced a series of solutions, not always coherent with each other, of considerable interest to themselves but apparently of very little interest to historians as such. The character of most of these answers (and perhaps the explanation of their lack of interest for historians) may properly be described as "assimilationist." The common characteristics of these assimilationist answers are first to seek out all traits of historiography that can reasonably be identified with or assimilated to the model of scientific explanation by means of general laws; then to make epicyclic modifications of the general-law structure of explanation to accommodate some of the more evident deviations of historiography from its pattern, always holding such modifications to the minimum; and finally wholly to prescind from some of the most evident traits of historiography on the ground that they are irrelevant to the quest for knowledge, understanding, and truth. The last procedure, which for present purposes is of the most importance, is illustrated by a passage in Morton White's *Foundations of Historical Knowledge*, a passage of special interest because among the practitioners of analytical philosophy White

alone is also a practitioner of historiography at a very high level
of excellence.

> The historical narrative, the extended story, is so large and ram-
> bling by contrast to the single sentence treated by the logician
> that any effort to treat it as a repeatable and identifiable pattern of
> language may give an impression of remoteness and distortion well
> beyond what might be felt by the historian who finds his causal
> statements cast in a single syntactical mold. On the other hand,
> the very qualities of narrative which might lead a historian to
> think that logical analysis distorts it are those that might inhibit
> a logician from trying to discern its structure. The complexity and
> variety of narrative, the fact that one story seems so different in
> structure from another, may give both the romantically minded
> historian and the classically minded logician pause. Yet the vast
> differences that human beings exhibit do not prevent us from
> X-raying them in an effort to discern the skeletal structure that
> each of them possesses. . . . History is a literary art as well as a
> discipline aimed at discovering and ordering truth, and if we
> neglect some of the narrative's literary qualities in order to clarify
> certain epistemological problems connected with it, our procedure
> is like that of the sane roentgenologist, who searches for the skull
> without denying that the skin exists and without denying that the
> skin may vary enormously in color, texture, and beauty.[8]

The equation here is at once interesting, dubious, and exemplary
of the assimilationist posture above described. Before presenting
it, by the addition of a couple of rather large epicycles, White had
already assimilated several common traits of historiography as
closely as possible to the general-law model of scientific discourse.
The quotation announces his intention to do the like with another major trait, the storylike character of much history writing.
But he knows this is going to leave him with a very large residue
of what historians write still on his hands. This residue consists
in part of matters that the analysis of historical rhetoric in this
article has called attention to. He disposes of this uncomfortable
residue by assigning it to history as "a literary art" rather than
history as "a discipline aimed at discovering and ordering truth."
In this connection his analogy with roentgenology is not wholly

fortunate. For it is at least arguable that the knowledge that history makes accessible is no more fully revealed by the mere skeletal structure of its narrative than the knowledge of the human head is fully exhausted by what an X-ray plate shows about its mere ossature. Just as it may be suggested that while the human head is partly a bony structure and partly (sometimes) a thing of beauty, it is also a number of other things, too, so it is possible to grant that history *is* a literary art while denying that all those aspects of history writing which White consigns to that function and that function alone are actually irrelevant to the function of history as a discipline aimed at discovering and ordering truth. It has been one purpose of the foregoing article to suggest some grounds for such a denial.

The mention of epicycles in the preceding paragraphs provides us with a clue to the dis-ease of analytical philosophy with historiography, a dis-ease so acute that it has become an intellectual disease which may be a prelude to a general and deep intellectual crisis. Epicycles suggest the Ptolemaic system of astronomy, and examination of the ultimate crisis of that system may by analogy help toward an understanding of the current crisis with respect to knowing, understanding, explaining, and truth that the study of historiography has induced in analytical philosophy. The crisis in the Ptolemaic system came in the sixteenth century, when it was destroyed by the Copernican revolution. For centuries before, it had been normal science. Following the terminology of Thomas Kuhn, it was structured about several paradigms, among which were (1) the earth is at the center of the cosmos; (2) the earth does not move; (3) the orbits of all heavenly bodies are circular; (4) the circular motion of each heavenly body is uniform in rate. These paradigms were invoked to support an area of pre-Copernican science far more extensive than celestial mechanics; and to save this science, the observed deviations of the planets from presumed circular orbits and uniform speeds were dealt with by an ingenious but exceedingly intricate system of epicycles, eccentrics, and equants. The Copernican revolution was initiated by Copernicus' allegation that this system could be greatly simplified by assuming that the earth was not at the center of the cosmos and that it moved around the sun annually and rotated on its own axis daily.

Certain facts about the Copernican revolution are worth noting in the present context. (1) Copernicus' own work by no means provided a wholly satisfactory solution to the difficulties it sought to deal with. (2) Although the third and fourth paradigms of Ptolemaic astronomy—those dealing with the orbit, shape, and speed of the planets—ultimately crumbled under the impact of the revolution Copernicus started, he had no intention of displacing them and in fact held firmly to them. (3) Copernicus' heliocentrism and geomobilism implied the destruction not merely of Ptolemaic celestial mechanics but of other large tracts of the science of his day; what he offered in place of what he destroyed was, however, unsatisfactory. In some matters he offered nothing in place of it, and in others he does not seem to have been aware that he had destroyed it, so that overall for a long time the old normal science provided better explanations of many phenomena than the Copernicans did. (4) For all the above reasons the marginal advantage of the Copernican over the Ptolemaic celestial mechanics was not at all clear, and the conservatism of those who continued to adhere to the older scientific paradigms for a long time is quite intelligible.

Let us now apply this analogy to the crisis that has confronted the analytical philosophers as a result of their explorations of historiography. Until and except for that confrontation, their paradigms—essentially the modes of rhetoric they ascribed to the sciences—provided them with a reasonably satisfactory way of understanding and rendering intelligible the syntactical structure and vocabulary of a language capable of conveying frequent increments of knowledge, meaning, and truth—the language of the natural sciences. From this fact of experience they assumed that all knowing, meaning, and truth can be incorporated into statements in their paradigmatic rhetoric and that nothing that cannot be reduced to that rhetoric can claim a place in the region of knowing, meaning, and truth. During their twenty-five year confrontation with historiography they have discovered one anomaly after another in the rhetoric of history, place after place where it appears to deviate from the language of the sciences. Their most general response has been to try to save their normal view of the nature of knowing, meaning, understanding, and truth and of the proper rhetoric for communicating them by constructing a complex structure of the logical equivalents of epicycles, eccentrics, and equants in order to assimilate to it as much of the rhetoric of history as possible and thereby save the paradigms which support that structure. This procedure has been less than satisfactory, because it requires them quite arbitrarily and without evidence to assign to many traits of the rhetoric of history an altogether aesthetic rather than a noetic function. This has been especially the case with respect to those aspects of the work of the writer of history which concern themselves with the telling of a historical story and with the disposition and arrangement of his evidence and the choice among alternatives, all connotative rather than purely denotative, for the communication of what he knows. The philosophers have proceeded as they have for the very good reason that to do otherwise would be to raise extremely perplexing questions about the nature of knowing, understanding, meaning, and truth to which, as of now, neither they nor anyone else has any very plausible answers.

One of the aims of this article is to suggest that nevertheless a paradigm shift which would raise such questions may now be desirable and even necessary. The first step would be to assume that the rhetoric of history, including much to which analytical philosophers assign only aesthetic value, constitutes an appropriate response on the part of historians to their commitment to advance the knowledge and understanding of the past as it actually was. There are no better reasons for rejecting this assumption than for making it; logically to reject it or to accept it involves decisions equally arbitrary. It has, however, a certain prima facie empirical plausibility; it is based on an uninvidious view of the consistent refusal of some of the very best historians dedicated to communicating the truth about the past wholly to adopt the rhetoric of the sciences. To start with this favorable assumption would provide room among the means of knowing for certain rules of historiography concerned with the advancement of knowledge, for which there seems to be no room within the present structure of knowing as the analytical philosophers conceive it.

It would by no means open the way for the sort of intellectual slatternliness that analytical philosophers rightly object to and oppose. On the contrary, it would assist in the introduction of some much-needed conscious intellectual rigor into regions in which rigor has often been sadly lacking or in which its presence has been due to the experience and temperament of particular historians rather than to thoughtfully codified professional standards of performance. But to do all this requires an acknowledgment and acceptance (1) that in some areas of human inquiry the pursuit of truth can be effectively carried on only by means of a rhetoric which diverges from that of the sciences and (2) that this is not wholly due to the peculiarities and perversities of those who pursue the truth in those areas but in part to the very nature of the terrain over which they must pursue it. Once analytical philosophers fully recognize that there may and indeed must be more than one style, one rhetoric, for communicating the things that are both knowable and communicable, and that the problem is not that of reducing all styles to one but of carefully investigating what style is appropriate to the particular problems of communication inherent in a particular kind of knowing, it will be possible to bridge the now ever-widening gaps that separate analytical philosophers, historians, and rhetoricians. They might then join in trying to discover whether a thorough exploration of historiography, the rhetoric of history, can teach them anything worth finding out about knowing, understanding, meaning, and truth.

3 /

The Historian and His Society:

A SOCIOLOGICAL INQUIRY —

PERHAPS

SOME years ago, Mr. Ved Mehta wrote for the *New Yorker* magazine a series of articles on the practice of history. They were based on the views expressed to Mr. Mehta by several eminent British historians, and reported with what accuracy who knows. Bearing the curious title "The Flight of the Crook-Taloned Birds," the articles seemed to demonstrate among other things

(1) That perhaps some English historians are unduly addicted to behaving in a fashion associated with a place on the other side of St. George's Channel called Donnybrook;

(2) That English historians must be intrinsically more interesting than American historians, since the latter achieve notoriety only through the occupancy or pursuit of public office while the former seem to stumble into it just by being themselves;

(3) That oral communication to an innocent-seeming Indian may not be the ideal means of formulating one's views on history for dissemination to a wider public.

What follows is an attempt to clean up only a small corner of the area that Mr. Mehta's broad brush so generously spattered. At one point he dealt with the views of Mr. E. H. Carr, expressed in a book called *What is History?* The title implies a modesty not wholly characteristic of the work itself, which with greater accuracy might have been entitled *What History Is.* As Mr. Mehta puts it, "In his book, Carr unhesitatingly held on to his belief . . . that all history is relative to the historians who write it, and all historians are relative to their historical and social background." "Quoting Mr. Carr ('Before you study the history, study the historian. . . . Before you study the historian, study his historical and social environment'), history was not objective (possessing a hard core of facts) but subjective (possessing a hard core of interpretation). Each generation reinterpreted history to suit itself. . . ." So much for Mr. Mehta. We might add another posy to the bouquet of quotations from Carr.

When "we take up a work of history our first concern should be not with the facts which it contains but with the historian who wrote it." The onetime shepherd of all historians in the United States, Dr. Boyd Shafer, former executive secretary of the American Historical Association and editor of the *American Historical Review*, instructed his flock that Mr. Carr's *What Is History?* was "the best recent book in English on the nature of historical study."[1] We historians then were practically bound by pastoral injunction to browse in the intellectual meadow that Mr. Carr had so generously provided us. Already, perhaps the reader may have inferred that I am in something less than perfect sympathy not only with the judgment of Dr. Shafer but with the statements of Mr. Carr, and with the point of view which they enfold. In this he would be correct.

Mr. Carr has formulated that point in another way. You cannot "fully understand or appreciate the work of the historian, unless you have first grasped the standpoint from which he himself approached it." Thus he says, in order fully to understand his *History of Rome*, one must know about Theodore Mommson's disillusionment with the liberal revolution of 1848. Fully to understand his *England under Queen Anne* one must know that

George Macauley Trevelyan was "the last of the great liberal historians of the Whig tradition"; fully to understand his *The Structure of Politics at the Accession of George III*, one must know that Lewis Namier was a continental conservative.[2] At this point in Mr. Carr's disquisition, I ground to an abrupt halt. It suddenly struck me that there were two early American Namierites, and that by a wild coincidence they were among the historians whom I had known best and longest.

The first is Professor Walcott, whom I have known for thirty-five years; the second is myself whom I have known for a bit longer. Professor Walcott is a Namierite by choice; and I had watched with awe the incipient Namierization of the early Parliaments of the eighteenth century from close in, when we occupied neighboring stalls in Widener Library. I am a Namierite by grace of a reviewer for *The Economist* who has admitted me to "the nuclear club whose first member was Sir Lewis Namier."

Since we were both charter members of the Harvard Chapter of the Teachers' Union back in the thirties, I take it that during his early Namierizing days, Professor Walcott was not a conservative. And, born in Cambridge, Massachusetts, he is a continental only in the eighteenth-century American, not in the British sense of the word. As for myself, I was once a member of the Grievance Committee of the Red-infested New York College Chapter of that same Teachers' Union, and of four academic colleagues who were invited to my wedding, three subsequently took the Fifth Amendment in the course of loyalty investigations. And I am not a continental either. I am a Cincinnatian. Now if to understand Professor Namier's history it is important to know that he was a continental conservative, to understand our writing is it equally important to know that Professor Walcott and I, two early Namierites, were *not* continental conservatives—or even just conservatives? If Namier's attitude toward society is the first thing that readers of his work need to know, what effect did my *ignorance* of his attitude have on me back in the thirties when, scarcely conscious of the fact, I became a Namierite?

And this brings us to another puzzle. Why should Professor Namier's politics strike Mr. Carr, no Namierite, as important, and me, a Namierite, as unimportant? The difference lies in the questions Mr. Carr and I are interested in finding answers to. Mr. Carr wants to know why Namier wrote a book like *The Structure of Politics at the Accession of George III*. For people with a taste for this sort of guessing game, amateur seat-of-the-pants psychologizing is less a vice than an unfortunate but inevitable consequence of raising the problem in the first place. I know this because I have had a try at the game myself in connection with Thomas More's *Utopia*. My early questions about *The Structure of Politics* were of a character very different from Mr. Carr's. They were as follows:

(1) What that is new does the book say about English politics in the middle of the 18th century?

(2) Has it got the story right?

(3) Can I make any use of the way *The Structure of Politics* was put together in the kind of work I am doing?

Suppose I had put those questions to Mr. Carr, and he had replied, "When you take up *The Structure of Politics*, your first concern is to know that Lewis Namier was a continental conservative." I fear my reply would have been, "Pardon me—would you mind answering my questions?"

Mr. Carr has stated his purpose in another way. It is "to show how closely the work of the historian mirrors the society in which he works." Now, if by the society in which he works, Mr. Carr means the vast tumultuous event-matrix of all human happenings during his lifetime, then like everybody else the historian mirrors it badly, because only a very small part of it can ever be in any one man's range of perception. The sector of human happenings a man is likely to mirror best is the one he is involved in most, the society or societies, the associations of men, in which he indeed lives and works.

The society of professional historians

We need not embark on an arduous and uncertain quest for the society historians work in. With great wisdom and perceptiveness it has been identified for us by the federal government; and annually the Internal Revenue Service reminds us of the facts of life. Crushed and bleeding from the embrace of the Iron Maiden, Form 1040, we seek among the cancelled checks for some surcease from pain, and we find: dues, American Historical Association; dues, Organization of American Historians; dues, Economic History Society; dues, Renaissance Society—deductible. Expenses: meeting of Midwest Conference on British Historical Studies—deductible. Subscription, *Journal of Modern History*—deductible; subscription, *History and Theory*—deductible. Depreciation of library, almost all history books—deductible. Share of utilities for space used in the house for writing history—deductible. The United States Government then has not a moment's doubt about what society I work in. It says that I work in the society of professional historians. And as a neighbor of mine used to remark, "What's good enough for Uncle Sam is good enough for me."

An inordinate amount of what has been said about historians and the history they write has gotten into stultifying tangles because no heed has been paid to the fact that preeminently the society which professional historians are members of, belong to, work in, is the society of professional historians. Nearly all the competent history writing done nowadays is done by professional historians, people who are trained in and live by the regular practice of history as lawyers live by the practice of law, physicians by the practice of medicine. In these matters the very first line historians draw—like lawyers and physicians—is the one that separates their particular community of professionals from the rest of the world who with respect to history or law or medicine are laymen. Yet in face of the massive professionalization of the writing of history, most people who have meditated publicly on the way history gets written have not seen fit to make any analysis, much less to make a serious investigation, of the effect on historians of their membership in a society of professionals. What I would like to do here is to suggest a few of the consequences of membership.

The most important consequence of entry into the society of historians is that the entrant is thereafter called upon to write history. To get history written is the only unique purpose of the society, the only trait that unmistakably distinguishes it from other similar societies. To get history written, not to get it taught. Academia itself usually makes teaching a condition of employment for professional historians, and since there are few other paying posts available to them, they teach willy-nilly, usually willy, but sometimes nilly.

The central institution of the society of historians is judgment by peers. He who enters the society of professional historians thereafter subjects himself to the judgment of the other accredited members of that society. This process of judgment determines the relation of the individual historian to that society which more than any other affects his chosen life work. It imposes on the varied individuals who are members of the society a common discipline by precept, and the other institutions of the society enforce that discipline.

One trait of judgment by historical peers sharply differentiates it from such judgment in the courts of law. The latter kind of judgment forbids double jeopardy. A verdict in favor of a man brought to trial on charges before his peers in a court of law is not subject to reversal at any future time by any authority whatsoever. The society of historians acts on a rule diametrically opposite to this—a principle of multiple jeopardy and unlimited reversal. At any time any historian may subject the life work or any fragment of the life work of any other historian to a judgment, and no statute of limitations runs against him. Thucydides has recently got into bad trouble. The historian puts himself forever at the mercy of the present and future members of his society each time he emerges from the enclosed comfortable womb of silence into the cold clattering public marketplace of print.

The subjection of what one writes to judgment by one's peers is not often pleasant, and the temptation to avoid it is strong. By not writing at all one can avoid it. But since the main object of the society of historians is to see to it that history gets written, it cannot tolerate evasion of this sort. To prevent it, the society in which historians work has adopted another institution of the English common law. Rather early, that law had to cope with an analogous problem. Unless a man would plead to the charges against him before his peers, he could not be judged.

To avoid the awkward consequences of this situation the common law employed a device called *peine forte et dure*. The *peine* was provided by weights which were piled on the recalcitrant to encourage him to face judgment. If he persisted in his obduracy, weights continued to be added until he either changed his mind or was crushed to death. The society of historians in its infinite wisdom has so arranged matters that the effective alternative to publishing and facing the judgment of one's peers is to be crushed to death professionally by the weight of their indifference. So for the historian, too, it is "plead or die," or in another aphorism "publish or perish." Of course, just as the man before the bar of justice may plead *and* be condemned, it is not at all unlikely that a historian will publish *and* perish; still the odds, however unfavorable, are better than no chance at all, and for the man who never publishes there is no chance at all.

The mechanisms of judgment by peers in the society of historians are numerous and varied, formal and informal, public and private, written and oral. We can deal only briefly with a few of these mechanisms.

It is, of course, in the learned journals that we find the most conspicuous and noisy mechanism for judgment—the book review section. Also most formal, most formidable and most effective in the short run, but, unfortunately, perhaps the least accurate and the least competent. Why formal reviewing in the learned journals of the historical profession in America is pretty bad would take long to explain, because part of the badness is rooted in the very structure of the craft, while another part is related to the character or rather a few characteristics, of American society as a whole. A third part of the badness is the result of remediable operating deficiencies of the professional journals which could (but probably will not) be corrected with inconvenience only to the editors of those journals.

One or two of the more obvious defects of the review columns of the journals as channels for judgment by peers, however, need to be mentioned. In the first place they move too fast. To a novice historian who with bated breath waits for two years after publication for the first review of his book, the notion that judgment comes too fast will seem ludicrous. What usually delays the review, however, is not the reviewer's deep thinking about the book, but his avoidance of thinking and writing at all about a book concerning which he does not feel he has anything sensible to say, or his mere laziness and insouciance. Moreover there are more reviewing journals than there are willing and able reviewers. Reviewing is an exacting, time-consuming, ill-rewarded skill likely to win the reviewer more enemies than friends, rarely undertaken by senior members of the society except as a favor to a friend, as part of a brawl with an old opponent, or more properly and I suspect more frequently as a part payment of the noneconomic dues they owe their profession. Finally the journals review only books, never an article, no matter how important that article may be. Nonetheless and despite the drawbacks and deficiencies of reviewing, the society of historians needs an evaluation however tentative of the output of its members, and the writing historian for professional, practical and psychological reasons does not want to wait indefinitely for the first shower of roses and/or dead cats.

Even before the long slow drizzle of reviews of a book is over, the more loosely-structured and, be it said, more reliable judgment by peers starts; and in the case of articles these judgments are the earliest ones. A useful formal and public mechanism of this kind of judgment is the footnote. It is a splendid and versatile instrument which serves many purposes besides its ostensible one—that of indicating where an author claims to find support for a statement. Among these purposes is the provision of a convenient location for the payment of scholarly debts. The instrument of payment is not in its form quite as fully standardized as ordinary commercial instruments, but it usually goes something like this: "For a fuller discussion of this point see Wallaby's solid article, 'The Decline of Possum Hunting in Dade County as a Criterion of Evangelical Revival,' *The Florida Journal of History*, 12 (1947), 12–17. Robert Ryerson's *The Possum as a Frontier Phenomenon: Myth and Reality* (Madison, Wis., 1959) is too general and too unreliable for use." The last part of the above footnote carries its own warning. Those little devices are not merely organs of praise but instruments of judgment, and woe is the miscreant bore who has inflicted his incompetence on an irascible judge with a footnote handy to hang him on.

Academic correspondence provides a private, indeed confidential, but highly effective mechanism of judgment. For example, in answer to an inquiry Professor A. receives the following letter from Professor B., who on other like occasions has proved to be a reliable source of information. "In connection with the opening you mention in Early Modern History, I have a few suggestions. They do not include Adcock, about whom you specifically ask me. His recent articles suggest that he is very suitably placed in his present job at Grand Guignol State Teachers."

The life of the professional historian is the life of teaching, silent study, work, and writing, interspersed with brief orgies of gossip. According to Adam Smith, where two or three businessmen gather, there is a conspiracy in restraint of trade. According to the apostle, where two or three gather in faith, there is the church. Where two or three historians gather, there is shop talk, and where there is shop talk, there is judgment by peers. It goes

on on the steps of Widener or in the New York Public Library or
the National Archives or the British Museum or the Bibliothèque Nationale. It goes on among members of the same department, and it goes on with somewhat enhanced intensity in
those innumerable meetings of groups with a shared specialization into which the society of professional historians finds it
convenient to fracture itself—the Central States Renaissance
Conference, the History of Science Society, the Conference on
British Studies, and so on. Here is just one brief sample to show
how it works.

"I have been so swamped with chores this semester I haven't
had a look at Frisbie's new book on the Scottish Parliaments."

"Don't bother."

The crucial judgments are considerably less casual, and the
most careful and painstaking of them take place in the confidential deliberations of *ad hoc* committees and departments of history dealing with appointments and promotions. The better the
department the more careful and penetrating the judgment.
This I have reason to know because it is my good fortune currently to be a member of the Department of History at Yale,
a society of able and conscientious professionals. I remember vividly a meeting of the department's permanent officers
some years ago. Should the department meet an offer made to
one of its able young members from another university by pro-
moting him to a position that gave him tenure? The small committee which had read all his published work and a manuscript
ready to submit to a publisher came in with a split vote. Others
had also done some reading. After two hours of wholly unacri-
monious debate, it was evident that the decision would rest on
a judgment of the manuscript. "Well," a former president of the
American Historical Association said wearily, "It looks like we
have to go and do some more homework." So over the next two
weeks some twenty-five of the better-paid members of the profession spent a very considerable number of man-hours reading
the manuscript and arriving at their tentative individual judg-

ments. They then met again for two more hours of deliberation before coming to their collective judgment. Thank God, judgment is not always, or even often, that expensive, difficult, and time-consuming.

Such then are some of the mechanisms by means of which a historian is judged by his peers from the early days of his apprenticeship until and even after his death.

The dedicated teacher

As a structured entity the machinery of judgment by peers in our society is awesome; I can imagine that, called to admire its intricate convolutions, however, some crude iconoclast might ask what purposes of any sort it serves. It serves as the foundation of two other primary institutions of our society. In the first place it establishes the pecking order. It operates as a rating device and develops a consensus among historians as to who's who and about how who he is.[3]

The pecking order along with the movements of demand determines the going prices of particular historians on the job market. To a considerable extent it determines what according to one's rhetorical preference may be called the allocation of the conventional rewards of Academia, the apportionment of distributive justice, who gets how big a piece of pie, or the division of the loot. There are, of course, other means, some proper and useful, some sordid, for augmenting the conventional rewards of Academia, but probably the surest over the long run is to write history favorably judged by one's peers. Granting exceptions, most of the cushier posts in history's corner of Academia are in the hands of historians deemed by their peers to have written competent history.

But—one can almost hear the pathetic sob—what of the dedicated teacher? The question is raised frequently—one who has heard it again and again may be inclined to say, *ad nauseam*. It has often been alleged that in the dealing out of loaves and

fishes, the provision of distributive justice, the apportioning of
the conventional rewards, or division of the loot adverted to
above, our society, the society of historians, commits chronic and
grave injustice by overrewarding the productive scholar who cannot teach for beans, and underrewarding the gifted teacher who
does not—this last to be said with an appropriately contemptu-
ous curling of the lips—"grind out research." This view of the
situation depends on a number of assumptions no less nonsensi-
cal for being almost universally accepted, one or two accepted
indeed by the very research scholars who are their intended vic-
tims, and who having assented to a false assumption find themselves logically pressed toward conclusions that they know are
absurd. An assumption of this last kind is the one which equates
teaching with classroom performance, and in its most extreme
form with performance before a group of students of considerable
size. This last view, reflected in the statement I once heard made
about one eminent scholar, "He is good in seminars, but he can't
teach," is too foolish to waste powder and shot on.

It is the more moderate view, the view that all important
teaching is done in the presence of pupils, that enjoys almost universal approval. Of course, to define teaching as the transmission
of knowledge and understanding by word of mouth in face-to-
face relation between pedagogue and pupils may be convenient
for some purposes, especially perhaps for the purposes of persons
who transmit knowledge and understanding in no other way.
Nevertheless, five hundred years after Herr Gutenberg's entertaining invention, such a definition has a somewhat archaic
aroma. There are three major formal means by which historical
understanding and knowledge are in fact transmitted to those
who seek knowledge and understanding: the reading of sources,
the reading of what historians have written about the sources
and about the works of other historians they have read, and the
hearing of a talk by a historian in which he purveys whatever
knowledge he has acquired by the two previously mentioned
means. It seems to me highly probable that most people with any

considerable amount of historical knowledge and depth of historical understanding owe the larger part of it to what they have read by historians rather than to what they have heard from them.

But surely, it may be said, the dedicated teacher who has a block about writing ought to receive rewards equal to, perhaps superior to, the man who publishes a bit and has a block about teaching a class. Since the issue is cast in ethical imperatives rather than actualities we can avoid dealing with the implication, quite possibly contrary to fact, that all the goodies, psychological and material, are showered on research historians, who are bad teachers, while the devoted teachers, who are not research historians, stand out in the cold, their pitiful pinched faces pressed against the window pane. But we must at least indicate that the proponents of the "dedicated teacher" canard have won a handsome propaganda victory. Somehow in certain circles they have put across the idea that practically all historians who do competent scholarly work are maundering bores in the classroom, and that they treat their students like gnats to be brushed off or, if the students are persistent and the professor short-tempered, like mosquitoes to be slapped at. Conversely the mere fact that a college teacher of history has published nothing is somehow transformed into prima facie evidence that he is so profoundly involved in teaching that he has no time to spare for turning out trifles in the research line. Unfortunately for its propagators this view has made relatively little headway in the society of historians, because the leaders of that society know it is pure poppycock. In the course of their careers they have known too many superb teaching historians (we here follow without accepting the usage which confines the term teaching to a face-to-face relation), who, stinting nothing in their classrooms or in their concern for their students, have yet done scholarly work of distinction. They have also known colleagues who published nothing, not because of their devotion to teaching but because of their wholehearted dedication to birdwatching, to billiards, to Old Overholt, to squalid in-fighting on the lower rungs of academic politics, or simply to providing their backsides with facilities for acquiring an appropriate middle-aged spread. Despite its well-nigh universal rejection at the better addresses in Academia, the peculiar myth that hopefully we have just buried has long flourished in some academic circles and is propagated with unchecked fungoid luxuriance in the shady academic demimonde inhabited by educationists whose dim view of research and scholarship is doubtless an undistorted reflection of the quality of their own professional efforts along those lines.

One last fallacy of the justice-for-devoted-teachers crusade (which, as often happens in crusades, occasionally nudges over into a witch hunt against the advancement of learning) needs to be dealt with. It is necessary to admit that some men who write good history are bad classroom teachers. Yet by their peers they are judged to be good historians. But does not equity then demand that the successful classroom performer who cannot write history also be judged as a good historian and enjoy thereby all the rights, privileges, honors and honoraria thereto appurtent? Let us examine this apparently equitable proposal more closely. First, how do we know whether the man who writes history is a competent historian? We know, because he has taken the pains to provide us with clear evidence readily and publicly accessible. If he who runs cannot read, at least he who will sit down for a few hours can read—and judge. The historian who writes can be judged on the basis of standards that have been set by the collective experience of his peers and by the achievements of the ablest members of the society of which he is a member. Who judges the competence as a historian of the classroom teacher, and by what standards is he judged? In the main he is judged by the undergraduate students who listen to his lectures, and by what standards God only knows.

We do know, however, if we will but recollect our own undergraduate days, how little our standards had to do with the teacher's competence as a historian. Is there one of us who does not recall having been enthralled in our early college years by a classroom teacher of history whom we later discovered to be a pretentious faker or a mere clown—*vox et praeterea nihil?* If in judging their peers the society of historians is inclined to have greater confidence in the kind of evidence that a colleague's writing puts in their reach than in the kind that his classroom teaching puts in their reach, it may be not only charitable but just to ascribe their preference to a sensible evaluation of the relative quality of the two kinds of evidence rather than to a dark conspiracy against competent classroom teachers. After all, aptitude in gauging the quality of evidence is one of the most highly treasured tricks of the historian's trade.

Moreover traits in no way germane to a man's ability as a historian may and sometimes do diminish his effectiveness in the classroom. He may have a high whining voice; he may be extremely awkward; he may not be a ready improviser; he may have an incurable and severe stammer; he may be terribly shy; he may be deaf and so on. If they are severe enough and numerous enough, such traits may disqualify a man altogether from classroom teaching, but they all speak entirely to his aptitude for oral communication and not at all to his skill as a historian. On the other hand it is hard to see what equivalent obstacles immaterial to a man's competence as a historian intervene to block the passage from spoken to written discourse. Surely there is no less need in oral than in written discourse for data coherently organized, relevant, and enlightening. And such a need is no less pressing in the *viva voce* than in the written communication of history. Therefore anyone who speaks history as it should be spoken ought to be able to write history as it should be written. Something of course may be lost in the writing—the pregnant pause, the ironic inflection, the delicate shrug, the telling gesture, the raised eyebrow. Still with the exercise of a little ingenuity verbal surrogates for these varieties of vocal and physical twitching can occasionally be found. And on the balance while not denying that some of the meat of the spoken discourse may be lost when

it gets set down in cold print, one occasionally wonders whether
the meat in question is roast beef or ham. So much for the dedicated teacher of history who never writes history.

The mills of scholarship

Our peers in the society of historians then judge us by what
we write and subject to *peine forte et dure* those who refuse to
produce any testimony on which they can base a judgment.
Thereby they aim to apportion the conventional rewards of
Academia in some more or less sensible relation to the quality-
cum-quantity of historian's published work. Presumably this is
the way the society to which we belong provides us with incentives to do our job, which is to get history written.

Incentives, however, are only important where the work to
be done is dull and unrewarding, but historical research and writing——! A swimming eye and an enraptured set of the face becomes practically mandatory as Parnassus heaves into view with
the Muses draped along its slopes and Clio herself doing *en-
trechats* at the apex. It is a mighty pretty picture, but that is all
it is.

A great deal of historical research and writing is stiflingly
dull and unrewarding work. The vision of the historian as a sort
of intellectual private eye, swashbuckling through a succession
of unremittingly fascinating adventures of the mind, can survive
only among those who do not destroy it by engaging in historical
research. In fact a large part of historical work is indeed like
detective work, like the dreary, patient, systematic, interminable
detective work that goes on in dozens of precincts and police
headquarters, following false leads down dead ends; compiling
large, uninteresting and frequently irrelevant dossiers; and ques-
tioning dreary and dull sources of information who (or which)
often provide not an additional fragment of a clue to what one
knows already.

If throughout this harrowing grind our historian has continuously burned with a hard gemlike flame, it is only because God endowed him more generously than He has endowed most men and most historians with the fuel of enthusiasm. Take a stroll some day where the historical researchers congregate in a great library. Note the number of scholars bowed over their desks, their heads resting on their arms. They are not at the moment burning with a hard gemlike flame; they are not thinking deep and exciting thoughts; they are sleeping off their ennui. Their task—the task of historical scholarship—has bored them not to extinction, but to a merciful though temporary oblivion.

Still the research ends, the working up of the evidence into a finished piece of history writing starts, and the historian at last tastes the pleasure of scholarly creation. Or does he? Well, if he has an aptitude at the management of evidence and a flare for vigorous prose, perhaps he does enjoy himself a good bit. But what if he has not? Then through sheet after sheet of manuscript, past twisted sentences, past contorted paragraphs, past one pitiful wreck of a chapter after another he drags the leaden weight of his club-footed prose. Let us draw a curtain to blot out this harrowing scene and turn to look at one of the fortunate few to whom the writing of a historical study is a pleasure of sorts. He writes the last word of his manuscript with a gay flourish—and he better had, because it is the last gay flourish he is going to be able to indulge in for quite a while. He has arrived at the grey morning-after of historical scholarship, the time of the *katzenjammer* with the old cigar butts and stale whisky of his recent intellectual binge still to be tidied up. He must reread the manuscript and then read the typescript and correct and revise as he reads. And he must, of course, check the quotations for accuracy of transcription and all the footnotes for accuracy of citation. Then he sends the fruit of his labor to a publisher: and if he is lucky, the publisher accepts it, asking only a thousand dollars or so by way of subvention to cover the cost of printing. In return for this benefaction the historian gets to read his handwork again in galley proof and yet again in page proof. And then comes the crowning indignity, when sick to death of his own best effort, he drains the nauseating dregs of historical scholarship; he has to read the damn thing again and prepare an index.

And then? And then judgment by peers. For the unfortunate on whom the verdict is unfavorable, any connoisseur of the review columns of the historical journals knows the delights in store for them. "Dr. Thompson has thrown new light—but not much of it—on one of the more trivial episodes in Italian diplomatic history." "Unfortunately Dr. Thompson has not taken the trouble to familiarize himself with the latest studies on this problem by Swedish scholars." "Dr. Thompson has not chosen to mention my study of Bergamese diplomatic documents, which perhaps he has not thought it worth the trouble to examine." "For an adequate treatment of Dr. Thompson's subject we will still perforce rely on the five magisterial tomes of Colavito and Gentile published in the 1820s." "Thompson's rather bold and unorthodox view on certain personal eccentricities of Adolfo V, the so-called Mad Duke, are by no means sustained in the more cautious and conservative studies of Best-Chetwynd, F. Hill, Spillane, and de Sade." And so on, as one undergoes the capriciously-timed drip-drip of reviews in the historian's society's version of the Chinese water torture. Under these circumstances the society of historians wisely hangs on to the stick of *peine forte et dure* and the doughnut of the pecking order to keep its balky members pacing the treadmill that grinds out historical research.

Those who cannot contemplate with equanimity the foregoing account of how the wheels of productive historical scholarship are kept in motion would argue that history produced under conditions of labor rather like those of the more satanic early nineteenth-century textile mills will be worthless. Can men with little taste for historical work really do anything worthwhile? The answer to this question is "yes." The notion may not make happy those generous souls who, confusing their wishes with actuality, believe that competence waits on dedication. It does not. There are lovable, enthusiastic, and inept oafs in our profession, and there are deplorable, nonchalant, and skillful idlers. When the latter are routed out of their sacks and driven to labor in the vineyard they always beat the former hands down in the judgment of their peers.

Judgment by peers

Listeners who have not been distracted by the rhetorical arabesques of the foregoing from their effort to keep clear the lines of argument may have noticed some traces of ambiguity and equivocation. The central purpose of the society of historians, it was pointed out, was to see to it that history got written. The function of judgment by peers was to establish a pecking order for the purpose of facilitating distributive justice. And the purpose of differential distribution of the loot was to hold before historians the prospect of material reward in order to persuade them to dig hard at writing history. Thus judgment by peers was made to seem one of the mechanisms in an integrated series all directed toward maximizing quality/quantity of historical output. Somewhat closer scrutiny has indicated that this is not a very accurate account. Quite evidently in the matter of encouraging historical scholarship the pecking order and the allocation of rewards are on the opposite side of the account from judgment by peers. By its terrors the latter prospect discourages publication. Hopefully the pecking order and the prospect of a good share of the loot offset the damage that judgment by peers has done. They work with it only in the misleading sense that an antidote may be said to work with its corresponding poison. Taken alone judgment by peers does not stimulate the production of historical scholarship; it retards and strangles it.

Then if the purpose of the society of professional historians is merely to get history written, the sensible thing to do is to drop judgment by professional peers altogether. This would not, of course, necessitate giving up the real stimuli to writing history. We would retain *peine forte et dure*, the pecking order, and the differential division of the conventional academic rewards. We would even retain judgment. Only the judges would not be a historian's professional peers. Republican historians would write history for Republicans to be judged by Republicans; organic gardening historians would write history for organic gardeners to be judged by organic gardeners, and so on, and we would hire a statistician, an econometrist and a theory-of-games man to solve the problem of slicing the pie.

Yet even though the incentive system just outlined would almost certainly release a great flood of historical writing, it is doubtful that the society to which historians belong would be willing to settle for it. Despite the fact that judgment by peers dams instead of releases that flood, the society of historians will, I suspect, cling to that institution to which all the rest are geared, and since it inhibits historians from writing, our earlier statement, "The purpose of the society of professional historians is to see to it that history gets written" is incomplete. Completing it is easy enough. One simply adds three words: the purpose of the society of historians is to see to it that history gets written *the right way*. In context "the right way" means "the way our society wants history written."

Although a rough consensus of the society of historians about the details of the right way to write history in fact exists, to describe and explain that consensus would take a good while. There is no doubt, however, as to the common opinion of our society about the *goal* of the right way. We want history so written that any one who wants to know anything knowable about the past can find it out; so that where knowledge is possible, it will also be present; so that wherever one seeks footing in the past, there will be as much footing and as solid footing as the careful, patient, and imaginative study of the surviving remnants of the past by men skilled in their craft can make available. It is to just one end that our society maintains its elaborate structure of *peine forte et dure*, judgment of peers, the pecking order, and the differential division of the rewards: that with the exercise of reasonable care and prudence whoever chooses to move about anywhere in the recorded past can find solid ground and not continually be tumbling into bogs, quick sand, crevasses, and pitfalls.

A couple of specific illustrations of the force of the rules of game—the guild standards, if you will—on professional practices and judgments of professional historians may serve better than general allegations to illustrate the way the society of historians polices its members.

Before the Second World War a bright young Englishman wrote a thoroughly competent historical study of an English county in the sixteenth century. For more than a decade he continued to write competent historical studies. He had started out as a Marxist. (It was stylish at Oxbridge in the thirties to be a Marxist. Radical chic is not an invention of the late 1960s.) Gradually a cluster of peculiar changes overtook the young historian, no longer so young. Once a Marxist, he turned into Tory when Toryism became modish. Once able to command the attention of his professional peers in England, later he commanded the attention only of lecture tour audiences and of uninformed readers of the *New York Times Book Review* in America. Once poor, he became rich. Once a professional historian of considerable parts, he became the fabricator of careless, sleazy, incompetent, widely sold potboilers. And his professional peers who had once paid respectful attention to the young Marxist paid disrespectful attention and then almost no attention at all to the aging Tory. Not because he had ceased to be a Marxist and become a Tory, not because, a former small seller, he became a big seller, not because, once poor, he was now rich. No, simply because he had broken the rules of the society of professional historians to which he had once belonged and on whose respect his self-respect ultimately depended; he had made himself into an unreliable hack. Professional historians had no occasion to refer to what he was saying about the past, because what he said was not worth referring to. So his later writings died a few months after they came off the press. As a professional historian he was in effect cut off in his prime—suicide or homicide or oddly a combination of both. In any case the society to which he had belonged, the society of professional historians, showed a remarkable capacity for conferring early mortality on an erring member and on all his later works. As a historian he is now a corpse with a pocketful of money, scarcely an adequate recompense for an early demise.

The second illustration is more edifying. It concerns a young scholar, Professor Jesse Lemisch, who proclaims himself a radical historian. He has recently published "Radical Plot in Boston (1770): A Study in the Use of Evidence," a twenty-page review of Hiller Zobel's *The Boston Massacre*.[4] Professor Lemisch's view is unfavorable to the book. He charges Zobel with "proof by dint of no evidence or contradictory evidence." Zobel argues, for example, that the mob in Boston was " 'controlled but in appearance unchecked.' " Yet the evidence says nothing of control and an abundance about excessive spontaneity. Further, "Zobel consistently avoids evidence against his case." His case being that the Boston mob was manipulated, he fails to follow up clues, imbedded in the evidence which he himself offers, that some of the Boston rioters were moved by a genuine sense of grievance, indeed perhaps by genuine grievances against the British troops. What he does with respect to the Boston mob he also does to the colonial leaders. He indulges in selective quotation. Thus John Adams's serious alarm at what in his own words he construed as "the determination in Great Britain to subjugate us" by military occupation is reduced by Zobel's omission of that quotation to mere " 'annoyance.' " Further, Zobel's " 'positive identification' " of rioters in 1765 is based on "information from indictments—to which the accused plead not guilty and were never tried—for a riot which took place" during 1764. And so on.

From a reading of the review, two points to our purpose emerge clearly. First, Zobel takes a view of the behavior of the American colonials slightly more jaundiced than that of George III, and some of Lemisch's animus in the review results from ideological hostility to a historical perception different from his own. This is clear from some of his asides, such as

> Can the lawyer [Zobel] draw from his studies of the preliminaries of a past American revolution no better "lesson" . . . than obedience, authority, the hard line. . . . It may be appropriate to remind the reader at this point that in the years following the Massacre such policies carried out by the people whom Zobel admires and on whom he relies for the greater part of his evidence precipitated revolution.[5]

With serious qualifying additions and amendments, I happen to draw from the recent "youth revolution" in the United States substantially the lesson of "obedience, authority, the hard line," which Lemisch finds lamentable. Moreover, in Lemisch's case casually and accidentally I have followed E. H. Carr's injunction, "Before you study the history, study the historian." Having done so, as a student of the sociology of knowledge, I can then understand Mr. Lemisch's review of Zobel's book as a manifestation of youthful academic malaise in the early 1970s.

But second, I am only a spectator of the society of the sociologists of knowledge. It is not the society I belong to. I belong to the society of historians, and my membership in it requires me to attend not to Lemisch's current socio-political postures in 1971, which I think will be ephemeral and which do not especially interest me, but to the substance of his criticism of a book about 1770. That substance, what he says about the uses of dubious evidence and loaded language, seems to me to leave Zobel with a good many tough questions to answer. If he cannot answer them, he or someone else will have to modify his account of the Boston Massacre not to satisfy *radical* historians, but to satisfy historians. That is what makes the note Professor Lemisch wrote on the copy of the review he kindly sent me almost touchingly wrongheaded:

> For Jack Hexter,
>   from a radical asking some conservative questions about evidence and proof . . .

The whole implication of Lemisch's review is that there are no such things as radical or conservative questions about evidence and proof. Historical evidence is slight or abundant, dubious or trustworthy. Historical proof is difficult or easy, adequate or inadequate. Evidence and proof are never radical or conservative. Rather, they are part of the common language in which historians communicate with each other, the common ground on which they stand or fall. They are part of the discipline which, soon or late, the society of historians imposes on *all* its members.

From the men who write history and are then dragged in fear and trembling before their peers for judgment we have made the traverse to the society of historians which in willing the end of solid footing in the past wills the means by which it is produced, and its quality policed—judgment by peers with all the pain it entails. *But the society of historians is composed of the very people it drags up for judgment. In effect the society of all historians in general wills the torments that each of them undergoes.*

Though many members of the society of professional historians would like to improve the efficiency of its institutions, odd as it may seem, not one, I think, wants to destroy judgment by peers. For however annoying it may be to historians as individuals, still knowing the deep-grained sinfulness of all flesh, they know very well that judgment by peers is what stands between them and slovenliness, pamphleteering, distortion of data, laziness, habitual inaccuracy, dullness beyond the call of duty, and a host of other evils which ultimately and cumulatively would mean the collapse of our society's morale, the frustration of its ends, and therefore, be it noted, the failure of all of us in our calling. Rousseau's conception of the general will as something different not only from the will of each but even from the will of all has sometimes been derided and often is misunderstood. I know of no better illustration of the meaning of the general will than its mode of operation in the society of professional historians in the matter of judgment by peers, where to achieve a recognized and acknowledged common good, by a general consent and working through general rules, the will of historians as members of that society imposes itself on the often tough and truculent individual wills of all its members.

The socialization of historians

The historical relativist and the *afficionado* of the sociology of knowledge profess to be profoundly impressed by the impact of society on historians. On one side, according to them, there are the sources—the unshaped, unsifted surviving records of the past. And on the other hand is the historian's Society with a big S, which is just about everything that goes on during the historian's lifetime. Society screeches and roars and hisses in the historian's ear. Each day it passes vividly and living before his eyes. It stinks in his nostrils, and pounds him on the head, and tromples his feet, and squeezes his hands, and tugs at his heartstrings, and turns his stomach, and kicks him, and pats him on the back. Of course, with his soul-filling experiences of his Society on one side and the scatter of colorless records of the past on the other, our historian simply impresses on the record whatever is most important or vivid to him at the moment in his current responses to his Society. One thing, however, he appears never to do: he never reads a book by another historian bearing on the historical problem about which he is concerned. In this respect unlike any professional historian for the past century, this Byronic character of the relativists' dream is an absolute unqualified individualist. The fact is that for all their talk about Society, the relativist and the sociologist of knowledge wholly disregard the impact on historians of that society—the only society—to which as professionals all historians belong, and thus they miss the true social character of historical work. They disregard the extraordinary extent to which the history that gets written is formed by the society of historians acting through, on, and in the individual historian.

Most of the history written by professionals works within a dual reference system. That system refers him (1) to the contemporary sources used by the historian and (2) to the work of other historians used by him, and he is obliged to certify his competence by referring back in his footnotes to the sources and the work of other historians. Under the strong safe cover afforded by this latter obligation the society of historians in arrayed battalions marches square into the work of each of its members. Where there is a "literature" on any subject which a historian deals with he is supposed to know that literature. But to "know the literature" is not to know all the books and articles related somehow or other to the subject. Some books and articles are obsolete, some are trivial and worthless. Some antiquated works will have fallen from the bibliographies and footnotes or, because of exemplary incompetence will never even have got into them. But the very tasks of genocide and infanticide which lead to this result have been performed for the historian by his society. Nevertheless the number of works by other historians consulted in producing a single monograph often runs into the hundreds, so Mr. Carr's precept "When we take up a work of history our first concern should be not with the facts which it contains but with the historian who wrote it," seems less a counsel of despair than an invitation to madness. In effect, by this point in the history of history writing practically all history is collaborative. The subjects which no historian has touched on before, on which no investigation, even tangential, has been attempted are negligible. Even if he repudiates all current views and regards all previous investigations as tissues of error, a historian must implicitly or explicitly counter those views and undermine those investigations. Even when he does not lean on the work of other historians he must specifically lean away from that work. And such drastic leaning away is the marginal case. The bulk of historical work involves modification rather than subversion.

If, from the beginning, a historian's writing is "socialized" by the necessary employment of the work of other historians, at the end it is "socialized" again through judgment by peers. The apparatus of judgment warns readers of areas of weakness, indicates areas of strength, points to what is old and decrepit, to what is new and deserving of attention. Finally and most important, the very prospect of judgment by peers socializes the writing of history while the historian is writing it. Knowing that his place in the pecking order, his share of the rewards, and his own estimate of himself, depend on that judgment, he takes pains to do those things his peers approve of and to avoid those that they condemn. What they approve is imaginative compliance with the rules which help to extend the area and increase the firmness of footings for those who seek knowledge of the past. I can only once more express my astonishment that the men who have talked most glibly about the conditioning of the historian by his society have never done at all what is here done rather badly: examine the relation between historians and the society to which they belong, the society on whose estimate of them, their level of income, their standing among their fellows, and their own judgment of their life achievement largely depend.

Dry cargo

In my penultimate observations I should like to indulge myself in the luxury of speaking in parables.

Once upon a time three men were considering going into the import business. Their names were Albert, Bertram, and Claude, or A., B., and C. They were inlanders who had never seen a freighter, so they came to a port to have a look around. The first ship Albert boarded was a miserable old tub. "What's this hulk for?" Albert asked. He was told it was to carry freight. Then he went below deck where he saw that the ship leaked at every seam and that there was three feet of water in the hold. Albert shrewdly observed, "Sea water will damage any cargo this wreck carries." And he was right. The second ship he boarded was in as bad shape as the first. "Sea water will damage what this wreck carries, too," he sneered, and he was right again. Then he visited another ship. He went down into the hold and he saw an inch of water in it. Being a clear-headed man, he thought as follows: "All ships have some water in their holds. Therefore on all ships the cargo suffers water damage. Therefore it does not matter what ship you buy cargo from." As a result of this brilliant syllogism he bought indiscriminately. Of course nobody in the market trusted his judgment, so even when he lucked into a good consignment he found no customers, so Albert or A. went broke. But among people not in the business, he became a sort of hero; and he was called by them an import relativist, because, they said, he had proved that all imports were relatively wet.

Our second man, B. or Bertram, was a more reflective type than Albert. He, too, inspected several freighters. Taking his clue from the seepage of seawater in all ships, he decided that freighters were apparatus for the collection of oceanographic information. A careful study of seepage would provide data on the nature of the waters which the ship was currently travelling, a sort of sociology of the sea, so to speak. This conclusion had drawbacks, however. On the view that the value of freighters lies in the contribution their bilge water makes to the sociology of the sea, the leakier the tub the better. If freighters are mainly important for their leakiness, why do the better operators take so much pains to make them as watertight as they can? Moreover, whatever the contribution the investigations proposed by Bertram might make to oceanography or the sociology of the sea, they were of no use at all to people who want to know which freighters carry clean, dry cargo.

And it was to just this problem of clean cargo that C. or Claude addressed himself. Being a man of drearily systematic habits, he kept lists of freighters and checked their holds on several of their returns to port. He also checked with other importers and with underwriters whose interest it was to learn which freighters took good care of their cargo. He knew that even the tightest ships ended their crossings with a little water in the hold;

but he also knew exactly how those ships were loaded, so although a bit of their cargo occasionally got damaged he rarely bought that part of it. Now he did *not* say that all imports were relatively wet; he said some were wet and some were dry, and that he could tell the difference; so the import relativists called him an absolutist and regarded him as naive. And the fauna and flora in the water that seeped into the bilge did not interest him very much, since what he really was concerned about was the quality of the cargo. So sociologists of the sea thought he was simple-minded and possibly a reactionary. But the other people in the importing line had a different name for him. They called him an old pro.

Here endeth the parable and here almost ends this sociological inquiry. To give a specious penumbra of legitimacy and relevance to my remarks on the import business I will finish with something about a shelf in a library. It is in the British History section. Adjacent to each other on that shelf are Francis Aidan Cardinal Gasquet's *Henry VIII and the English Monasteries* (1888), and Geoffrey Baskerville's *English Monks and the Suppression of the Monasteries* (1937). Now the historical relativist will smile tolerantly at this juxtaposition because it shows, does it not, what happens when you turn a Roman Catholic and a skeptic loose on the English monasteries and their dissolution? You get just the difference of opinion you would expect, Gasquet all sympathy and Baskerville all sneers, and it is all relative to the social prejudices and prepossessions of the two historians. So it does prove, does it not, that Mr. Carr was right after all, and that when "we take up a work of history our first concern should be not with the facts which it contains but with the historian who wrote it"? The sociologist of knowledge, however, observes that the differences are very instructive; since they provide clues to the ideologies current in the 1880s and the 1930s, although of course they tell you nothing for sure about the 1530s. Finally, perhaps an old pro comes by the shelf of the library whereon Gasquet and Baskerville repose. Out of long habit he runs his eyes further down the shelf. There they light on four massive volumes, *The Monastic Order in England* and *The Religious Orders in England*. He observes as he examines that the master of those volumes, the late Regius Professor of Modern History at Cambridge, has taken the infinite pains that the historians are trained to take in order to keep his cargo free of the seawater of current ideological conflict. Therefore, the old pro does not need long to decide that those volumes rather than Gasquet or Baskerville carry the goods he wants to buy. In fact, all the professional traders have transferred their custom to the late Regius Professor while between occasional and increasingly rare charterings by enthusiastic and incompetent amateurs, Gasquet and Baskerville rot away at the dock. And, of course, it does not matter at all that the late Regius Professor of Modern History at Cambridge, Dom David Knowles, was a Roman Catholic priest and a Benedictine monk. Although paradoxically, in the context which at the moment concerns us, that it does not matter at all is what matters most of all.

4 /

History and the Social Sciences

THE place of honor given it on the program of the quinquen-
niel International Congress of Historical Sciences suggests
that the relationship of history to the social sciences is a currently
pressing strategic problem for historians. The special reference to
quantification in the topic assigned to me suggests that numbers
are a crux of that problem. On the other hand one of those back-
ward glances at the record to which historians are professionally
prone does not suggest that we take these suggestions very seriously. For more than a hundred years now clamant voices have
urged that the time was ripe for historians to make the strategic
move that would adjust their discipline to some then current
version of the social sciences and for at least a hundred years that
move has been linked with the use of quantitative data.[1] This
iterated clamor of over a hundred years' duration, and as insistent
now as ever, does not indicate that any of the strategies hitherto
proposed have achieved sweeping success. And, granting the
dangers of extrapolation, statistically the auguries for impending

A report presented to the Thirteenth International Congress of Historical
Sciences, Moscow, U.S.S.R., August, 1971.

success are not reinforced by the record of a century of continuous failure. The intellectual disaster that would have followed had historians adopted any of the grand strategies actually proposed, as well as the stultification suffered by historians who have had a grand strategy inflicted on them, willy-nilly, both suggest that the trouble lies not in the actual relations between history and the social sciences, but in the notion that those relations are amenable to a grand strategy. Actually some competent historians have used some social science and some quantification, just as others have used other human activities—systematic theology, philosophy, sports, meteorology—as tactical or logistic aids to help them understand human doings, intentions, and sufferings in the past. It is hard for them to listen patiently to homiletics urging them to do what they are currently doing, or to do it by a Great Leap Forward, which they know will land them flat on their face. Many of them forget that not so very long ago they were neophytes who believed in some Great Leap Forward. They also forget how tempting it is, for the young, faced by the wearisome nuisance involved in learning how to gain any understanding worth the trouble about the past, to believe in a strategic Great Leap Forward that will soar above the nasty little tactical problems with which as working historians they will have to spend most of their lives.

It is easy, then, to understand the recurrent yearning for a single great strategic solution to the problem of the relation of history to the social sciences. It is equally easy to see that, despite the yearning, in a century no such solution has emerged and none is in sight. Perhaps it is inherent in history to defeat all grand strategies. Why should this be?

The disaster has two components.

(1) The nature of records of the past. For and to a historian the records of the past are his *data*, what is given him. Historians may find data their predecessors missed, but they cannot create them. If the evidence is too rough and coarse and full of gaps to use it on, a grand strategy for dealing with historical evidence is

of no use. Only by prowling among the records of the past can a historian learn what they are like and what questions they can be made to answer. Very often he finds that no strategy whatever can wring from the fragments that have survived answers to the questions that it purports to deal with.

(2) The catholicity of history. A priori, anything knowable about men as such is possibly of interest to a historian. The potential utility of the social sciences for a historian is therefore all-encompassing. Their actual utility is limited by the limitations of the records he encounters. The gap between the potential and the actual is enormous, and it increases rather than decreases as the sheer mass of social science knowledge grows. As it grows, not only the possibility but the utility of actually knowing it proportionately diminishes. Historians, excessively concerned like Alice's White Knight to be "provided for everything," far from being equipped for the quest for historical truth often seem engulfed in a useless clutter—a beehive in case there are any bees about, spiked anklets for their horse in case he should run into sharks. Like the White Knight too, perhaps because they share his excessive preoccupation with the dubiously relevant, such historians often seem to be ill-seated in the saddle.

For historians, these perdurable obstacles to a grand strategy have been reinforced in the past generation by changes in the social sciences. As never before social scientists are consulted and paid for their advice by men of affairs in both business and government. This *success d'estime* has coincided with (1) an increased employment of increasingly sophisticated mathematical tools, and (2) the creation through polling, censuses, tests, and data collection agencies of quantitative information precise enough to use the tools on.

Ocular, even quantifiable evidence of the reorientation of the social sciences is ready to hand for anyone with access to the old *Encyclopedia of the Social Sciences* (1930–35) and the new *International Encyclopedia of the Social Sciences* (1969). In the latter are dozens of articles on the mathematics used in the social sciences to which there are no corresponding articles at all in the older encyclopedia. Moreover scores of substantive articles that in the first encyclopedia were innocent of any quantitative symbols more sophisticated than dates in the second are packed with mathematical formulations wholly beyond the grasp of primitives like me from a more innocent era. A quantitative change has indeed become a qualitative one.[2]

All the more need, it would seem, for a grand strategy for making this new social science knowledge available to historians. Yet is is impossible for the same reason that made such a strategy impossible a generation ago, only the situation is even more hopeless. The proliferation of the social sciences and their mathematization have put an embracing command of them even further beyond the means of historians. Fortunately the new methods in the social sciences and the uses to which they are put have actually diminished both the incentive for an embracing strategy and the need for tactical devices to bring them within the grasp of historians. Of some slight interest to a very few historians, they are of practically no interest to most of them. They give much attention to the short-range forecasting of some of the effects of alternative actions within margins of error acceptable to the actors and presumably to those acted upon. That is, the social sciences have been directed toward the needs of men responsible for deciding the current policy of institutions—administrative, political, business or academic. They have met some of those needs by creating large or carefully sampled information inputs, by keeping those inputs abreast of current information, and by frequently revising their forecasts to conform to shifts in the output probabilities that the revised record of inputs entail. They have thus in effect contrived approximate equivalents of laboratory conditions and of the almost perfectly controllable containers in which physical scientists have done most of their experimental business at least since Lavoisier. In all this they were beaten to the draw by the insurance companies that for a long while have had to bet all the time on their forecasting skills.

With marginal exceptions all the operations of this group of social scientists are beyond the means of historians and useless to them. Historians cannot create data inputs that do not happen to have survived in the records of the past; and records before the early nineteenth century from which data full enough to warrant refined statistical treatment survive are rare and capriciously distributed.[3] Here where recent social science methods require a controlled opening in their containers, the data of history are ineluctably closed. Further, the past is closed; what happened unalterably happened, however hard it occasionally may be to figure out what did happen; while the future is open, it has not yet happened. It has to be forecast, it cannot be found. To forecast the outcome of the American election of 1970 is important enough to some people that they will pay social scientists for advice on how to do it; the rewards currently available to historians for forecasting the election of 1968 are exiguous. The precision of social science prediction varies inversely to the length of its time axis and to its geographical range. Keeping the axis and the range short improves the social science surrogate for a container. It improves forecasting by keeping out the unanticipated convergences and consequences of human activity. Such convergences and consequences cannot be kept out of the past because they have already happened. Recent social scientists "close" their containers with a *ceteris paribus* clause, which simply does not count the unanticipatable catastrophe. It is like the exceptions and "acts of God" clauses in insurance policies. Historians cannot play this game; an historian who will not count the French Revolution because it was unpredictable does not earn the golden opinion of his colleagues. Where social scientists can at least simulate closure, the past and therefore history is open. Although in lieu of the quest for an illusory grand strategy the problem of tactics in relation to some developments in the social sciences is worth a little of a historian's time, that time need not be spent in the area where of late those sciences have been most conspicuously successful. The conditions of historical investigation renders what is happening in that area of some interest to only a few historians. Historians who have most seriously tried to do in history what with some success some social scientists have done by new methods have built a strange instrument called counterfactual history. Its relevance to historical investigation seems to vary inversely to its sophistication and theoretical elegance. This result does not bode well for the gains to be anticipated for history from the arduous and ardent pursuit of those new methods. Most of us will easily find things to do with our time more useful or more entertaining or both.

USEFUL DODGES / What we have just noted is not grounds for despair but an antidote to it. Despair usually results from apocalyptic and millenial expectations, not from realistic appraisal. The latter begins when historians abandon the notion of a grand strategy and undertake the more modest quest for tactical instruction that will help them over the rough terrain of the surviving records of the past. Systematic tactical instruction to apprentice historians in a few techniques of quantification may be desirable on the same grounds that instruction in reading documents is already deemed desirable. All historians encounter documents in their engagements with the records of the past. Teachers, therefore, train novices to read and explicate them. To fail to do so is to leave young historians weak and unprepared in the face of what they will encounter sooner or later.

It now appears that almost all historians will sooner or later encounter numbers. Some novices may come to the study of history already trained, some may come with "good hands," that enable them successfully to manage without fumbling the numbers that come their way. They can do without special training. But many will come with neither previous experience nor "good hands." To deal with the data they will encounter they need to know at least the ABCs of numbers. It is going to take a while to identify what the ABCs are, and a while longer to figure a good way to teach them. The whole thing is a mean little tactical problem worth solving and possibly soluble, although we had better expect a good many failures before we achieve partial success.[4]

No equivalent pedagogic ABCs for the social sciences is even dimly discernible. Since there cannot be a grand strategy for coping with the many unpredictable tactical and logistical problems which the social sciences might help them solve or at least recognize, historians in their ignorance may often miss lines of inquiry more rewarding than the ones they actually follow. What are they to do? What historians badly need is not an impossible grand strategy but a quite possible small bag of tricks that will direct their attention to social-science knowledge that they can use on the record of the past.

Several useful dodges suggest themselves, and I am sure there are others that I have overlooked. If my terminology here seems raffish, I intend it to be so. For decades the area that concerns us has been the target of pompous programatics, inflated verbiage, big empty promises, and high-sounding claptrap. Merely to de-escalate the nonsense will be a service to sanity and sobriety. To this end I have adjusted the dignity level of my language to that of the notions they are intended to convey. The dignity level is low; the notions, however, may be useful.

The five tactical patterns that come to mind are (1) stargazing, (2) vagrant earflapping, (3) stackstalking, (4) crisscross shoptalking, and (5) suit-to-cloth cutting.

(1) As to stargazing, a dozen or so incontestable geniuses have systematically applied their minds to one or several of the social sciences; they are the stars. Adam Smith, de Tocqueville, Marx, Weber, Durkheim, Freud—it is possible, but difficult, to get through college without encountering their names. If they did not always come up with correct answers, they always asked exciting questions, and went about finding the answers in exciting ways. Honing one's wits on the works of a genius is worth doing in any case, and these particular geniuses angled in on men in their relations to society differently from the way historians do.

For minds not so credulous as to be gulled into astrology by it, stargazing is certain to be rewarding.

(2) Unfortunately most of the stars are dead. They do not afford a hot line into more-or-less current social science. So stargazing needs to be supplemented by vagrant earflapping, a most casual tactical maneuver, pleasantly slovenly, recreational, therapeutic, and sometimes profitable. It requires aimless reading around in the upper-middlebrow periodicals like *The Times Literary Supplement, Commentary,* and *The New York Review of Books.* Such journals pride themselves on being "with it" or "hip." Currently fashionable names and notions in the social sciences ultimately show up there, because most of the contributors to this sort of journal are compulsive name-and-notion droppers. Reading this sort of stuff is not necessarily less recreative than reading detective stories or science fiction; it provides more fodder for chic intellectual chit-chat; and for scholars with mild insomnia it is likely to be a more effective soporific. At worst such reading is not likely to be a serious waste of time. This procedure works best in lands that do not enjoy the benison of censorship. Even in those that do, however, the stupidity of the censors and the hired indignation of the intellectual apparatchiks permit useful clues to slide by.[5]

(3) If, in a journal read for recreation, either a name or a notion looks at all interesting, then via the card catalogue in the library one can pass beyond earflapping to the third tactical pattern—stackstalking. For stackstalking a scholar needs access to a library that classifies and shelves its books on topical principles, and lets scholars loose in the stacks. One simply goes to the place where a book to which one has been alerted by stargazing or vagrant earflapping is shelved and takes a look at it and a few of its neighbors. Since stargazing, vagrant earflapping and stackstalking have no specific aim, the best guide is idle curiosity and a desire to be entertained. One is more likely to be able to call to mind what one has found entertaining. And being able "to call to mind" is the hoped-for yield of the three tactical patterns. The

historian who practices them is more or less littering his mind with oddments in the hope that some of them may come in handy someday. Unless he finds them interesting, there is not much chance that he will remember them when they might actually be of some use to him. If he really wants to be a historian, however, he must not let his curiosity transform a recreation into a total preoccupation. If he does, he risks becoming a fairish dilettante social scientist at the cost of being no historian at all.

These three tactics are not related to any particular historical inquiry; they patently build in considerable timewasting. But then, it may be a bad idea to make a perfectly efficient machine the model for a historian's activity. Historians who come closest to such efficiency seem either to blow cylinders or to burn out bearings and grind to a permanent halt in their tracks, or else to tear at a splendid clip through monotonous territory to utterly dull and boring destinations. Building a little freakish inefficiency into the activity of being a historian may yield an overall gain.

(4) The fourth tactic, crisscross shoptalking, is more specifically purposeful than the first three and is likely to be a little more efficient. It works best in a good university with competent and sociable men in the social sciences. It also works best for a historian who has practiced the first three tactics. From them he gets a clue that one of the social sciences might help him make better historical sense of the records that currently engage his attention. He needs to find out whether anything in that social science actually does offer help, what the help is, where to find it, and whether it is worth the time and effort needed to gain access to it. Often he can find all this out fast by talking shop over lunch with a friendly neighborhood social scientist. At least little is lost in the process. One has to have lunch anyhow; people usually enjoy being asked for their expert opinion; even if it does not yield much, crisscross shoptalking offers as pleasant a way to pass a lunch hour as other forms of academic chatter. If one's first choice does not come up with anything useful, one can always try another lunch companion.[6]

(5) None of the preceding tactics demands systematic training in any social science; cutting the suit to fit the cloth does. It presupposes prior acquisition of the cloth. One systematically studies a social science and then seeks out historical problems to which it can be applied. This is a viable procedure. It is the way economic history is done nowadays. But economics is a social science unique both for the extent and the tightness of weave of its theoretical fabric. A historian who cuts his historical suit to fit the cloth of any other social science will find himself more skimpily clad in a garment less likely to protect him from the chill of ignorance and vacuity.

I do not claim that the five tactical patterns just described are novel, only that they are effective. That many historians have indeed found them effective does not create a strong presumption that they should be abandoned in favor of more sophisticated, elaborate, and systematic tactical ploys. Because they are easier to adapt to the varied unpredictable needs, interests, and abilities of individual historians, they are likely to meet those needs better than any standard course of instruction would. They will certainly meet them better than any course of study grandiosely claiming to offer a grand strategy to provide historians with the grasp of the social sciences that will equip them for their subsequent work. Any such claim is hopelessly naive or palpably fraudulent.

THROUGH HUMAN EYES / Does not that awesome quantifying device, the computer, and its complement, the Computer Revolution, drastically alter the historian's relation to quantification and thus affect the very nature of his discipline? Obviously,
(1) The computer is here to stay.
(2) The exploration of its applications is moving fast.
(3) For historians even the applications already in use have altered some ways of doing things drastically and made many hitherto undoable things not only doable but done. The phrase

"Computer Revolution" does not carry those germs of hyperbole that infect many uses of the term "revolution" these days. The computer enables historians to work effectively with large bodies of demographic, political, and economic data including census records, election returns, roll call votes, and banking records, hitherto too cumbersome to manage satisfactorily. It assists in graphic presentation of data. It makes content analyses of legislative debates, diplomatic exchanges, private letters, and memoirs. When the data are adequate and suitable the computer will sort them, classify them, and perform statistical operations on them with freedom from errors no man can achieve and at a speed that a thousand men working together could not attain.

To avoid what on the analogy of Kremlinology and astrology might be termed computerology, to avoid, that is, apocalyptic prophesy based on utopian hopes or primitive and uninformed fears, I shall be concrete and deal only with what actually has been done with the computer in the area of my own specialization. *Enterprise and Empire* by Theodore Rabb[7] is the only currently available work on the Tudor and Stuart period based on computer use. A sample set of one member is not statistically significant, but that is the only sample there is.

According to Rabb, from an economic backwater in 1550, England became "the leader of European commerce, industrial and overseas expansion" by about 1680, and in 1630 "all the foundations for that position had been laid." Rabb's book is about one of the groups "who made this transformation possible,"[8] the investors. To determine the social orders from which these men came, the absolute and relative numbers from each order,[9] "the size and relative importance of their investments, [and] their motives . . . ," Rabb turned to the computer because, "with over 6,000 people to be located and disentangled, even the easiest counting procedures would have been far too laborious and inaccurate if attempted by hand; and more complicated calculations . . . could never have yielded reliable results."[10] To cope with his data Rabb relies on two major capabilities of the com-

puter, data processing and mathematical operation, the former
to sort out investors classified by social order, the latter to count
them and to compute the percentage of the membership of each
company in each order. In both areas the computer makes feasible inquiries otherwise too costly in time and labor. Of the
sophisticated mathematical operations that the computer can
perform Rabb makes no use because his information has built-in
gross margins of error that render them sterile.[11] Any computation in his study could be performed by an eleven-year-old child.

The encoded data in *Enterprise and Empire* is based on the
9,000 names of investors in joint stock companies, overseas enterprises, and privateering, and/or members of Parliament from
1575 to 1630. Each name is coded for social order, for membership in Parliament and dates of membership, and/or for membership in thirty-one companies and dates of initial investment in
each.[12]

After processing and considering his data, Rabb arrived at
the key conclusion of his work. It concerns the role of gentry investment in the work of English expansion. He says:

> From the Court and from adventurous gentlemen brimming over
> with projects and enthusiasm came the momentum that trans-
> formed a series of commercial undertakings into a great national
> enterprise. In ideas and encouragement alone they contributed
> more than can be calculated from their numbers or investments.
> . . . In financial support . . . they helped substantially to amass the
> enormous funds necessary to surmount the first few hurdles before
> tangible results could be achieved.
>
> Hardly any returns were received on these investments. It
> could be said that most of the sums simply had to be wasted before
> the extremely difficult early stages of development were passed.
> And yet, viewed as a national effort, they were of course not
> wasted. . . . Vital experience had been gained, and the interest and
> determination had been aroused that were to bring spectacular
> successes in the next decades. During this pioneer stage, it was
> essential to marshal as much of the nation's resources as could be
> found. And here the gentry's role was crucial. It was precisely in
> the least financially profitable ventures that their money was

invested. . . . In both monetary assistance and inspiration the gentry's participation was vital to the foundation of England's empire.[13]

This passage elegantly illustrates the difficulties in transit between the quantitative information that the computer actually gave down about gentry investment and the qualitative assertions Rabb feels impelled to make about the role of the gentry in English expansion. Such assertions may be warranted on other grounds; but Rabb's quantitative evidence is ambiguous, and but feebly underprops his assertions. The heart of that evidence lies in two of his tables. The first is a table of "Companies in which gentry totaled at least 25 per cent of classified membership,"[14] the second of "Relative size of gentry and merchant investments in companies to which both classes contributed."[15] Not merely to render the data more immediately accessible, but because looking at them separately obscures their interrelations the two tables are conflated here. *Together* they are the heart of the matter: the number and social order of the investors *and* their estimated respective investments. The juxtaposition of the tables shows how different each table looks when viewed in conjunction with the other.

One can get the effect of seeing each table separately by covering the other half of the conflated table at the double line. Thus a quick glance at the left half of the conflated table seems to confirm at least one of Rabb's statements: gentry investors had a remarkable talent for betting on losers. Frobisher and Fenton, Gilbert, Gosnold, Guiana, Hudson, Newfoundland, Northwest Passage, Providence Island—they were all money going out and little or none coming back. Even the enterprises that ultimately resulted in enduring settlement—Virginia and Massachusetts Bay—were but poor things from the shareholders' point of view. But that table hardly sustains Rabb's belief that "the vital experience, the interest and determination that were to bring spectacular success in the next decade" had their source in Elizabeth's reign, "despite the appearance of almost total failure" which a

COMPANY	Number classified	Gentry members	% Gentry among classified members	Total capital	Provided by gentry and other non-merchants*	% Provided by gentry and other non-merchants	COMPANY
Africa	38	30	78.9	7,100	5,600	78.9	Africa
Baffin				9,000	1,100	12.5	Baffin
Bermuda	151	56	37.1	90,000	33,400	37.1	Bermuda
Cavendish	4	4	100.0	20,000	20,000	100.0	Cavendish
Drake				40,000	16,200	40.6	Drake
East India				2,887,000	415,700	14.4	East India
Frobisher & Fenton	97	47	48.4	28,000	14,000	50.0	Frobisher & Fenton
Gilbert	134	72	53.8	2,000	1,100	53.8	Gilbert
Gosnold	5	4	80.0	1,500	1,200	80.0	Gosnold
Guiana	92	78	84.8				Guiana
Guiana Company				5,000	4,400	88.7	Guiana Company
Guiana Venturers				75,000	67,100	89.5	Guiana Venturers
Hudson	24	9	37.5	3,000	1,200	39.1	Hudson
Irish	680	180	26.5	100,000	26,500	26.5	Irish

Mass. Bay	82	26	31.6	5,500	1,700	31.6
Minerals	75	36	48.0	7,000	3,500	50.7
Mines	56	26	46.4	34,000	16,400	48.2
New England	68	57	83.9	30,000	28,700	95.7
Newfoundland	50	13	26.0	20,000	5,200	26.0
New River	31	11	35.5	18,500	11,900	64.3
North-West Passage	307	81	26.4	12,600	9,000	71.7
Plymouth				7,000	1,200	16.7
Privateering				4,400,000	770,000	17.5
Providence Island	20	17	85.0	14,000	11,900	85.0
Virginia (1606–24)	1,252	560	44.7	200,000	94,400	47.2
Virginia Venturers				50,000	25,000	50.0
Weymouth	5	5	100.0	1,500	1,500	100.0
Other Ventures	340	143	42.1			
TOTAL	3,511	1,455	41.4	8,067,900	1,587,900	19.6

* The gentry as here classified include peers, knights, and other gentry. The "other nonmerchants" form a statistically trivial category. In all instances except Drake's enterprises and that of the Virginia venturers capital "provided by gentry, etc." is assigned or imputed according to the ratio of investors who were gentry to all investors.

casting of the account in 1600 would have revealed. The enterprises listed from before that date in the lefthand table were rare
and small; they involved few persons either as investors or participants. More important, it is to misunderstand the temper of
Elizabethan adventurers to imagine that they saw anything very
glorious in dying on ice on the Arctic tundra, or in sinking at
sea without a trace, or in coming back to port with a crew of sick
scarecrows and nothing in the hold in return for the time and
money spent. In this matter the Elizabethan's lust for fame and
glory has a strange resemblance to the modern American's much
lamented worship of the bitch goddess Success.[16] There is little
to show that Gloriana, who survived by always winning, and her
merry crew had much use for losers. And of the experience in exploration of which Rabb writes, very little can have been gained
from men so few of whom survived, or in colonization from men
none of whom survived, to tell their tale.

This result, so much at odds with Rabb's conclusion, requires us to uncover the right hand table to see if it may resolve
our perplexity. As a statistical experience this is rather like turning a sharp bend on a road through rough hill country and having
two spectacular peaks, as overpowering and dominant as twin
Mount Shastas, suddenly rear up before one's eyes. The lesser of
these economic giants is the East India Company, the greater is
privateering. Together the two absorb 90 per cent of the overall
volume of investment from 1575 to 1630, and privateering alone
commanded more than half the total capital. The third largest
enterprise involved only one-fourteenth as much capital as the
East India Company, less than one-twentieth as much as privateering. Of the investment capital of the gentry, nearly three-
fourths went to the East India Company and privateering. The
gentry put over four times as much money into the East India
Company, almost eight times as much into privateering, as they
did into the next-ranking Virginia Company. Yet neither of these
investment pinnacles appears at all in the lefthand or "gentry"

table, because in neither of them did the gentry make up 25 per cent of the investors.

To rank various overseas and maritime enterprises by the *percentage* of investors who were gentry creates an illusion. Suppose instead we rank them by the *number* of gentry who were investors. Then the East India Company and privateering catapult from eighteenth and nineteenth position to second and third.[17] The gentry did dominate several small and unsuccessful overseas enterprises that yielded no return, but more of them invested in the East India Company and in privateering than in any other overseas enterprise except the Virginia Company. Both privateering and the East India Company were highly profitable. From 1575 to 1603 for the gentlemen who put *five to eight times as much money into privateering as into all Elizabethan overseas enterprises in the left-hand table,* the "sea dogs" won fame and glory with a 60 per cent profit thrown in, a sort of Elizabethan gentleman venturer's answer to the Panglossian dream of the best of all possible worlds.[18]

How does one translate quantities into traits? What quantities register the "enthusiasm" of any particular social order for overseas enterprise?[19] There were 3,810 merchant investors and only 179 peers. Does this mean that the peers were about one-twentieth as enthusiastic as the merchants? Surely not. From 1558 to 1641 there were altogether only about 380 English peers, so that by such a criterion if the whole peerage had invested, it would still have stood only one to ten against the merchants in "enthusiasm." Actually a far higher proportion of peers than of any other order, fully fifty per cent, put money on the line to support English expansion between 1575 and 1630, as compared to one gentleman in fifty.[20]

There is a third major feature of the investmentscape, the Virginia Company. It is horizontally that it dominates the scene. It is not a peak, but an overpowering massif, because its base of investors is *hors de concours,* especially its gentry component.

Between 1575 and 1630, more gentlemen invested in the Virginia Company than in all the other overseas ventures in the table taken together. Almost all the investors entered the company between 1609 and its collapse in the 1620's. Thus the Grim Reaper beat the company to some of the gentry on Rabb's list. Nevertheless, just about half the gentry who invested at all put something into the Virginia enterprise.[21]

Between the years 1575 and 1630 the East India Company, the Virginia Company, and privateering dominated investment in overseas enterprise. Far more than half the gentry invested in no imperial enterprise except one or more of the Big Three, which together absorbed about nine-tenths of the capital that gentlemen put into such enterprises. A *gestalt* of the investmentscape to which the Big Three are peripheral obscures rather than clarifies our vision, since they are most that there is of it. They dominate the imperial investment field; yet each of them is so different from the other two and the relations of the gentry to each so divergent from its relations to the others as to nullify the notion of the typical, the average, the large and the small with respect to gentry investment.

This may be close to the heart of Rabb's difficulty. One of the matters he was most concerned to do was to discuss the small investor. The common sense antonym of "small" is "large." Properly informed, the computer could have sorted the small investors from the large ones in Rabb's list in a flash, and he would have known how many of each there were. There was not, however, enough data on the dimensions of individual investment to give the computer adequate information. Had he considered instructing the computer to do the job, Rabb would have discovered that domination of the investmentscape by the Big Three made it hard to tell the computer where he wanted it to draw the line between "large" and "small." After all the median investment of less than £50 in the Virginia Company would not have been nearly enough to buy a gentleman a piece of the action in the East India Company, where £200 was a minimum investment.[22] Enforced consideration of this difficulty would have alerted Rabb to the pervasive ambiguity that afflicts his study because he did not decide what he meant by a small investor or a large one, and as a consequence meant different things in different contexts.

For example, wherever one draws the line between a small investment and a large investment, is a man's investment large or small simply in terms of the pounds, shillings, and pence he invested? At the polar extremes a reasonable judgment is possible. Sir Thomas Smith is a member of the Levant Company, an investor in the Baffin and Hudson ventures, a director of the New England and Spanish Companies, a governor of the French, Northwest Passage, Muscovy, Bermuda, Virginia and East India Companies,[23] and it was rumored that he had put £20,000 in the last.[24] If he is not a large investor, the set is empty. At the other end of the spectrum is a London livery man who subscribes 2s. to Virginia, and never invests in any other imperial overseas enterprise the rest of his life. If he is not a small investor, that set is empty. Between the obvious extremes, however, our troubles begin—and perhaps never end. For example, except for courtiers and officials, Sir Edward Sandys is the only gentleman in a list of 560 recorded as investing more than £50 in the Virginia Company. Then is £50 a "small" investment? Well, it is one quarter the minimum price of admission to the East India Company— not big. It is 25 per cent of what Lord Sydney spent on his outfit for a Christmas masque in 1603—a trifle. It is one-tenth of the annual income of that minor country gentleman, Oliver Cromwell, a sizeable sum for him. And for a host of clodhopping Devonshire gentry, it is a whopping amount, the whole annual income of some of them.[25] "The small investor" turns out to be a fellow at once highly elusive and excessively elastic.

Before we attempt to set out some valid inferences about the use of the computer in history to be drawn from the preceding case study of *Enterprise and Empire*, it will be well to clear up a few invalid ones. (1) Most obviously, the computer is not responsible for any confusion in Rabb's study. It answered correctly the questions put to it. Therefore no exorcist rites by obscurantist historical witch doctors are in order. (2) None of the criticism above should be translated: "This is to show what happens when a brassy young whippersnapper steps in where elderly angels like me fear to tread." Rabb has been modest about the trying and complex job he has attempted. He has indicated the limitation of the computer for achieving his ultimate purposes, and he has searched out and marked with warning lights the numerous pot-holes with which the inadequacies of the record have pocked the road he has traversed. For his courage in undertaking his inevitably risky pioneering exploration he deserves nothing but praise. Pioneering helps those that follow after, not only by its rare successes, which point the ways to go, but also by those more frequent and less fortunate endeavors, which warn of other ways not to go.

In *Enterprise and Empire* Rabb saw his data in two perspectives. He saw them from very close up, and that made him conscious of the potholes that he encountered along the way to data encoding. He took many precautions to prevent them from throwing him off the path altogether. If his encoding or input perspective was microscopic, his output perspective was telescopic. He saw the vista produced by the computer's output after it had processed his almost 9,000 entries—a panoramic view, so to speak, from an enormous distance. But as those who have looked at mountains know, such a view may create illusions. Soaring peaks and great massifs in the furthest distance look no more formidable than steep hillocks and flattop mounds closer in, and from very far off are indistinguishable from them. How can one avoid or at least decrease the danger of errors of judgment that these two perspectives are likely to generate? Perhaps the easiest way is to familiarize one's self with the historical terrain by strolling about it with one's naked eyes open and up.[26] The naked human eye is anything but a flawless optical device, yet there are great dangers in closing it too long or in the wrong places. If one does so, one's image of the world may become very peculiar indeed. One must be very wary lest one tell the computer to homogenize one's data in processing it. So instructed, the computer will obey orders. But as milk is not homogenized in nature, the realities behind Rabb's data were not homogenized in the relevant past. To understand how things actually were one needs to contemplate the cream and skim milk separately.

The computer is a magnificent aid to research with dazzling potentialities for historical investigation. They are so dazzling that they may adversely affect the vision even of a wary historian who seeks to exploit them. When a historian computerizes he may unawares be afflicted wth "computer eyes." The computer does what other statistical operators sometimes do to data. If care is not taken, it homogenizes them as ordered, and "computer eyes" is but a virulent form of an already identified statistical disease that we may here christen "homogen eyes." The carriers of these diseases are not the tools men use but the men who use them. What historians see with "computer eyes" or "homogen eyes" are still human beings and human doings and sufferings. To avoid or correct distortion historians occasionally need to look at the past in a very old-fashioned way with human eyes. They fail to do so at peril of error for themselves and disaster for their discipline. For when historians forget to look at the past with human eyes, history will cease to humanize.

THE PROBLEM OF RHETORIC / The social sciences and quantification with or without the computer pose no strategic problem for history. They pose a large number of tactical and logistic problems, specific and detailed. To these problems, as we have seen, no general rule or principle applies. To social scientists, history poses a series of similar problems, best dealt with, perhaps, by the crude devices described earlier.

Given their recent orientation toward natural science models and toward quantification, in their relation to history the social sciences also confront at least one common problem of grand strategy, the most conspicuous symptoms of which are recurrent difficulties in the matter of language and word use. Given the nature of their objects of study, to most natural scientists it does not matter what it is like to be those objects. To a natural scientist the questions: "What is it like to be that electron?" "What is that oyster's conception of his place in the world?" simply make no sense, and it would be absurd for him to raise them. With respect to the objects of his studies, a historian is often impelled to ask such questions as "What was it like to be an eleventh-century French villein? a seventeenth-century English aristocrat? What was Louis XIV's conception of his place in the world? what Hammurabi's?" Such questions not only make sense to him; he cannot wholly evade them. But that kind of question cannot effectively be answered in the strictly denotative vocabulary of the natural sciences. This leaves present-day social scientists in a dilemma. Their aspirations lie in the direction of the natural sciences; the objects of their study, on the other hand, are those of the historian: men and groups of men in their aspirations, intentions, doings, and decisions. Social scientists are impelled to cast their discourse about men in a value-free natural-science rhetoric, even though that sparse rhetoric sometimes renders understanding of the love and hate, the dread and faith that move men not clear and deep but shallow and opaque.

Perhaps it is their desire to break free of this dilemma that has lured social scientists in the West into recurrent flirtations with Marxism and Freudian psychology. Both profess to be scientific ways of dealing with man. Yet the vocabularies of neither observe that strict neutrality necessary in the natural sciences. Unlike "density," "wave mechanics," and "Brownian movement" the terms "bourgeois mentality," "exploitation," "reactionary feudalism," "sexually repressive," "compulsive," and "anal erotic" do not evoke an emotionally neutral response. Marxism and Freudian psychology enable some social scientists to eat their cake and have it too, to profess allegiance to value-free science and yet to use a vocabulary that is shot through with value tintings. But Marxism and Freudian psychology are an inadequate intellectual diet. Nowhere have social scientists of their own free will kept strictly to the one or the other.

Those who have found that Marxian and Freudian solutions to their language problem demand greater intellectual sacrifices than they are worth have tried, perhaps unconsciously, an alternative tactic of evasion. Values, they concede, are constituitive elements of all but the most trivial levels of human behavior. Therefore they must necessarily be among *the objects of investigation*, when social scientists inquire into such behavior.[27] But while the objects of investigation, the value systems, are necessarily subjective states of consciousness, *the investigations themselves* and the reports on them remain or ought to remain wholly objective. This tactical move neither escapes the problem nor copes with it. The very language in which values systems are "objectively" described is itself irremediably value-contaminated; the value-tinting cannot be scrubbed out of it.

The nonsterility, the value impregnation of language is epidemic in the discourse of the social sciences and is bound to affect the import of what social scientists say. Shall we call the last phase of Hitler's policy with respect to Jews, as the Nazis did, "The Final Solution," or, as the Nuremberg Tribunal did, "genocide," or shall we call it "the massacre without the forms of justice of six million people"? Should we call the military action of 400,000 troops of a large nation on the strife-torn land of a small East Asian country "support of the legitimate government," "a policy war," or "imperialism"? Should we call the unresisted crossing of the borders of a small central European state by 600,000 unwelcome troops "comradely assistance," or "intervention," or "invasion"? How does one neutralize such terms as "policy war," and "imperialism," as "intervention" or "invasion"? How does one choose between them?

The last example strikingly illustrates a common phenomenon that frustrates the most conscientious value scrubber. Even when one replaces chilly terms like "imperialism" and "invasion" with cozy warm ones like "support of the legitimate government" or "comradely assistance," the value imputation somehow slips back from positive to negative. Too many acts of support and of assistance like those just described, and when they see the terms "support of the legitimate government" and "comradely assistance," people will read "imperialism" and "invasion." One does not change pig-liver sausage into *paté de foie gras* by relabelling the tin.

The infusion of value into social scientific rhetoric is a subtle and insidious business, and it happens all the time. Consider the terms "generalization," "interpretation," "objectively," "narrative," "humanistic," "test." None of them carry venerable distinct value markings the way "courage" and "traitor" do. They are all ambivalent or neutral. Put them together, with a few other neutral terms, and one gets the following italicized adverbial phrase:

"Insofar as history elects to strive *for objectively tested generalizations rather than only literary narrative or humanistic interpretation. . . .* " Even without that give-away "only," it is evident that the author here takes a dim view of historians who by electing "literary narrative or humanistic interpretation" rather than striving for "objectively tested generalizations," choose not to reach for the social-scientific brass ring on the intellectual merry-go-round.

The above illustration is in two ways *ben trovato*. (1) It occurs in the new *International Encyclopedia of the Social Sciences*, a compendium firmly oriented toward the mathematizing value-free natural sciences and away from history; (2) it occurs under the title: "Values, The Concept of Value," where its author propounds the tactic of keeping the rhetoric of the social sciences value-free while dealing with value systems by treating such systems "objectively." It is a happy circumstance that in the article proposing that particular tactic the inadequacy of the tactic itself should receive so striking an illustration.

The illustration is well found in another way, too, since it points, a little shakily perhaps, to the very traits of history that makes it so problematical for the social sciences—history's concern with what the author calls "literary narrative or humanistic interpretation." I would prefer to call it the appropriate rhetoric of history, when historians try to tell what it was like to have been Another. Those social scientists whose interest most often imposes a like requirement on them share the historian's awareness of the problem and, aware of it or not, demonstrate its existence in their work. So it is, for example, with the anthropologist whose "emphasis tends to become qualitative rather than quantitative" as he "seeks to construct a coherent over-all picture of the institutions of the people being studied."[28] That is, as he tries to tell what those people are like and what it is like to be them. Some who will read this essay will also have read Ruth Benedict's *Patterns of Culture*. If so, they may recall her skillful "over-all pictures of the institutions" of the Zuni, the Kwakiutl, and the Dobu. Without explicitly making a value judgment in those pictures, Miss Benedict left a wholly effective impression of how like peace-loving socialists the Zuni were, how like imperialist, conspicuously wasteful capitalists the Kwakiutl were, how like paranoid antirational fascists the Dobu were. We may reasonably doubt whether Miss Benedict was entirely just and faithful to the record in writing what came out so patly as a fable for the 1930s. Indeed her fable shows how hard it is to navigate between the Scylla of the rush to judgment, on which she came to grief, and the Charybdis of pseudo-*wertfreiheit*. The channel is narrow indeed, and perhaps cannot be gotten through completely unscathed. Still, the chances of coming through may be slightly enhanced by knowing that Scylla and Charybdis are there.

Two points, however, are beyond reasonable doubt:

(1) Problems concerning what individuals or groups of men have done or do, that is, problems of human behavior, are not wholly separable from questions about what such individuals and groups were or are like and what it is or was like to be them.

(2) Discourse about what people are like is radically un-scrubbable; efforts to clean out all value-tinged words simply re-move the color and the lines which, if one is to present a just and faithful picture, one cannot do without.

The dilemma of the social sciences lies at the interface of their relations with history and the natural sciences. Their aspiration to the value-free rhetoric of the latter conflicts with their inextricable involvement in the value-charged rhetoric indispensible to history, when history aims to communicate justly and faithfully what it is like to be Another.

An unconditional allegiance to a rhetoric free from value coloration deprives social scientists of that half cake which is not only better than none but also better than the whole cake of *wertfreiheit* which is sure to afflict them with chronic intellectual indigestion. There are human actions to which the vocabulary and rhetoric of responsibility, obligation, and conscience are irrelevant and human actions to which they are not only relevant but indispensible. These kinds of actions are so intertwined in living that attempts to effect a severance of them or to transform one into the other both trivialize discourse and dehumanize the discourser, making him into either an insufferable prig or a moral imbecile. Despite occasional theoretical statements to the contrary, practitioners of the two oldest humane disciplines, history and law, have always known this and acted on their knowledge. To the extent that the social sciences are strategically overcommitted to the value-free rhetoric of the natural sciences, they need to know it, too, and to effect the orderly general withdrawal and realignment of thrust that this knowledge suggests. Consequently history, which is the way men ordinarily give shape to their experience, poses not just a series of disparate problems of tactics and logistics for social scientists, but also a single massive shared strategic problem.

In the last few paragraphs I hope I have at least gotten into the target area where that problem lies. It is in the region of rhetoric. I am not quite so arrogant as to believe that I have a solution to the problem. I do have a notion of where to look for a solution. Its location is suggested by my previous emphasis on the concern of historians for just and faithful communication. It is more precisely defined in a few sentences by the late Garrett Mattingly. He notes that it does not matter at all to the dead whether they receive justice at the hands of succeeding generations. But to the living to do justice, however belatedly, should matter.[29]

To do justice is to render a judgment. An inference can be value-free because logically the premises entail the conclusion. Judgments about men cannot always be value-free; many of them are inherently acts of evaluation. Thrust judgment out of discourse about men through the front door of logic, and it immediately flies back through the window of rhetoric, a window that cannot be closed if we are to discourse at all about the human dimensions of men, about what, as men, they are like. To the historian it is important to do justice to any man that they humanly encounter in the record of the past. Not to be concerned with justice to one or many so encountered is to diminish not their human stature but ours. And so "to the living to do justice, however belatedly, should matter."

Since social scientists cannot wholly neglect the human dimension of humanity, a purely nonvaluative "natural scientific" rhetoric is inherently out of their reach. They can, however, not necessarily *faute de mieux*, be constantly alert to find *les mots justes*, and to avoid *les mots injustes*. Then their doomed effort to avoid responsibility for their language by a retreat into the natural scientists' quantified realm of the wholly value-free would give place to a fully conscious assumption of responsibility for their language as a moral and vocational obligation. Though in their work social scientists do not have the choice not to judge at all, they need not and ought not think that the task of finding justice once and for all is their ultimate end. Rather, since in the very nature of things the requirement of judgment and justice is locked into almost every nontrivial investigation or inquiry they undertake, they could try to do justice as a continuous process. Then the quest for a *wertfreiheit*, at once absolute and unattainable, would cease to be their ultimate goal. Limited and qualified it would survive in explicit creative tension with the perdurable concern of social scientists, as of all men, with justice.

Then a cleavage that threatens to widen into an abyss separating the generations of social scientists in my own country might become a bridge joining them. The disengagement and detachment of an older generation of social scientists, that to the young sometimes appear to verge on hard-hearted indifference, would be joined fruitfully with the moral concern of the younger generation, which now too often resolves itself into soft-headed mindlessness and myopic violence. Between detachment and engagement the continuous quest for a right and reasonable balance can and will never be easy, but as a noble philosopher who sought such a balance once said, "All excellent things are as difficult as they are rare."

As I conclude, I am more sharply aware than I have been throughout this paper that their full force, such as it is, applies only to a fraction of the historians and social scientists to whom it is addressed. For that fortunate fraction its imperatives are easy and require little boldness. Only the unforgivably self-serving or craven need reject them. To those, all of whose ultimate conclusions and many of whose immediate judgments are imposed upon them, willy-nilly, from higher headquarters by the monopolists of the instruments of violence, its arguments cannot fully apply. To historians and social scientists alike in this situation, who seek, however tentatively and cautiously, to win some footing of intellectual freedom for themselves and their fellows, we more lucky ones can only express sympathy for their misfortune and admiration for their courage. For the rest, and I hope they are few, who batten and fatten off the yield of their own sycophancy, for them it is hard to feel anything but pity—and contempt.

5 /

Doing History

To undertake a general characterization of recent historiography implies on the part of him who attempts it either a breadth of reading superhuman in its comprehensiveness, or a willingness to generalize (subject always to the correction of those who know better, other, or more) on the basis of reading more or less desultory and random. The present writer falls into the second category. His reading, indeed, has been more rather than less desultory, because he reads slowly and sacrifices much possible reading in order to write—equally slowly; more rather than less random because he lacks both the good sense and the impulse to order it systematically. Because of the impressionistic character of the remarks that follow, they will be accompanied by no reference to specific historical works. The unsystematic reading on which they are based would unintentionally but inescapably impart to such references an invidious character. Moreover, the sole possible validation of the general applicability of such remarks is a consensus of response from other historians: "In general that is the way it looks to me from where I stand, on the basis of such reading as I have done." On achieving or failing to achieve such a consensus the listing or mention of the books that any particular historian has read would have little effect.

Having made these reservations, I would venture two propositions:

(1) Never in the past has the writing of history been so fatuous as it is today; never has it yielded so enormous and suffocating a mass of stultifying trivia, the product of small minds engaged in the congenial occupation of writing badly about insignificant matters to which they have given little or no thought and for which they feel small concern.

(2) Never in the past have historians written history so competently, vigorously, and thoughtfully as they do today, penetrating into domains hitherto neglected or in an obscurantist way shunned, bringing effectively to bear on the record of the past disciplines wholly inaccessible to their predecessors, treating the problems they confront with both a catholicity and a rigor and sophistication of method hitherto without precedent among practitioners of the historical craft.

To document either of these dramatically opposed (but not mutually exclusive) propositions is unnecessary; evidence for both ought to be notorious enough to all who are actually engaged in the professional practice of history. One side of this well-known and paradoxical situation in historiography is the consequence of a condition which prevails throughout the academic world; the other side results from an internally generated shift in the canons of excellence maintained by professional historians. "The poverty of history"—the low yield of intellectual nourishment provided by much of the enormous output of historical writing—is a function of an explosion of demand so powerful as to set at naught the feeble attempts to maintain quality control over supply. The explosion has been a multiple one, and is extrinsic to the development of the historical profession. It is a correlate of the population explosion compounded by the concurrent inflation of demand for higher education. It has occurred in all lands where the gross national product has made feasible the investment in expansion of academic plant (building and grounds) needed to encompass the surging hordes of youth in lecture halls and classrooms. Having provided space for the multitude, the entrepreneurs of education have then had to find warm bodies capable of radiating to it higher education or a reasonable facsimile thereof. To attract these bodies a system of adequate rewards became essential, and also a means for differentiating rewards. In the postwar years, in most lands, religious orthodoxy, genteel or proletarian origins, racial purity, adherence to the locally-favored metapolitics, deferential subservience to academic superiors, and nepotism, all lost ground to publication of research as the basis for such differentiation. Aware that both climbing the greased pole (vertical mobility) and finding a cosier berth (horizontal mobility) depend on "productivity," as we say in industrially-oriented societies, the historians, like all other subspecies of the academic, began to produce in appalling quantity, and to seek outlets for their product in print. Whole legions of new historical journals were founded, university presses multiplied like fruit flies, but with fewer interesting variations, ostensibly to meet some deep-felt needs of the consumers of historiography, but actually in large measure to meet the far deeper felt needs of its producers. Their latent as against their manifest intent has been the advancement of bibliography, not of historiography. For the reasons just set forth, research which once would have found its appropriate place alongside the accompanying rejection slips at the bottom of a drawer or the back of a file cabinet, and have received in the end no more than a limited manuscript circulation among the immediate family of its producer as a memento of the dear departed, now issues by the ton from the press at forced draft and is shamelessly exposed to public view.

This accounts for the first branch of our paradox, the essential levity that underlies the pedantic solemnity of so much that passes for history writing today. It also poses for historians a professional problem worthy of far more serious thought than it has yet received: how in the world do we deal discriminately and in a time-saving way with this appalling mass of stuff? The problem will soon be compounded by the development and application to historical bibliography of the resources of elaborate information retrieval systems. As near as one can make out, such systems will be at once highly sophisticated at the level of taxonomic selectivity, and quite stupid at the level of qualitative discrimination. They will be able to pick out all the articles on any subject whatever, and wholly unable to say which, if any, of them are worth five minutes' attention. Their very competence at directing a researcher *to* all the recent literature in any field will compound his already staggering problem of picking his way *through* the field without sinking up to his neck in the dreary morass of wasted words. An attack on the problem of quality discrimination more persistent, systematic, and concentrated than any made so far should have a high place on the agenda of the profession. The old informal devices for finding one's way to what is good in current historiography are inadequate to the present situation, and a search for a way to provide historians with a reliable quality indicator, a sort of historiographic *Guide Michelin,* is overdue.

Although evidence for the second branch of our paradox is abundant and far more palatable than the evidence for the first, agreement about the remarkable advances in the historian's craft and the superiority of some of its yield is less certain. This (again paradoxically) is due to the very conditions indispensable to that advance. For one of its prime conditions has been the mastery by some historians of intricate skills which are difficult to acquire and of which very few historians formerly possessed more than a rudimentary knowledge. These skills often have to be brought to bear on a record which yields the data they require only reluctantly and in return for a very large outlay of energy and ingenuity. Historians nevertheless have to get along with these data because they cannot get along without them. They have to do so in demography, economic analysis, linguistic and content analysis, and voting behavior, to mention but a few instances. But the very cost in energy of pursuing historical truth along one or another of these rocky roads often produces a psychic deformation typical of the specialist. Historians so engaged sometimes overvalue the truth they pursue and unduly depreciate the value of truths that other historians find along other roads, partly because they share the common human failing which leads men to exalt the activities that have engaged their energies above those that have engaged the energies of others.

Yet those not numbed by overindulgence in the surfeit of bad historical writing and not overaddicted to their own exclusive recipes for excellence should be aware of the extraordinary abundance of work of very high quality that historians are producing these days in almost every field in which they are working. This abundance is in part the result of the emancipation of many historians from a number of old encumbrances. They no longer have to cope with several awkward presumptive commitments with which their predecessors in the nineteenth and early twentieth century had to deal. First, they have been freed of the stifling and stultifying effect of the positivist rules of historical method. These rules, based on what was wrongly conceived to be the method of the physical sciences, had led many historians to a sterile compendiousness, or more frequently to the concealment of their inevitably hypothetical and tentative generalizations under a bushel that hid the actual character of historical investigation from others and, more unfortunately, from themselves. The virtue of historical positivism was to commit the historians, as never before, to a scrupulous concern about the verification and veracity of their statements of fact, but the cost of that virtue was high. It consigned Clio to a conceptual virginity that was scarcely becoming in a lady of her ripe years, and made covert indulgence in what was stigmatized as "theorizing" seem more than a touch raffish. Nowadays, explicitly and in full consciousness of what they are doing, all but the most naive historians venture hypotheses, explain the data they assemble, and offer generalizations aimed at rendering the interrelation among those data more intelligible. One no longer hears about historians merely gathering facts which thereupon obligingly "speak for themselves."

Second, historians have been able to cut whatever filiation their discipline once had to substantive philosophies of history as represented by such metahistorians as Hegel, Marx, H. S. Chamberlain, Spengler, and Toynbee—philosophies which claimed that through the study of the whole past, history provided the key to the *whole* meaning of man, past, present, and future. Historians sympathetic to the metahistorical enterprise in general, although not necessarily to the work of any particular metahistorian, once tended to seek and hoped to find the meaning of their limited inquiries within the framework of some agreement on the whole meaning of the total past to be attained in the future, a final universal history to which they presumed they were making contributions. Historians unsympathetic to the enterprise, and they were the large majority, were pressed all the harder into the cramping positivist corner, because they conceived of all historical generalization on the model of the grandiose farrago of the metahistorians, and fled as far as possible from it. The deflation of positivism on the one hand and of the substantive philosophy of history on the other—a long slow deflation—has now freed historians from the sense of being confronted with an ill-fated choice, the disastrous alternative of bringing the frail bark of their investigations to shipwreck either on the Scylla of the one or the Charybdis of the other.

Intelligent criticism has reduced both positivism and the substantive philosophy of history to methodological absurdity, equally futile and preposterous modes of dealing with the data available to historians, chimeras to which no historian need pay heed, except insofar as he happens to be interested in the history of systematic intellectual error of a sort similar to astrology, heptascopy and phrenology. This emancipation from two divergent and equally stultifying commitments has had a further healthy effect—to provide intellectual elbow-room, so to speak, for the development of a philosophical critique of history writing as a unique significant form (the phrase is Mrs. Sheila Johann-sen's) of the species of human enterprises that have the capture and communication of truth as their prime object. As yet, however, historians have made little use of this elbow-room. Of this, more later.

Finally, historians have been able to renounce, if they chose (perhaps have had to renounce, even if they did not choose), the overdemanding conception of their function that required them to demonstrate that all their work was immediately germane to and provided clear directives for dealing with the current problems, dilemmas, and crises of the contemporary world.[1] Unless they wish to, historians no longer need claim that history has a specific present-day mission—the creation of a nation, the triumph of a class or a culture, the guidance of progress—of which they are the prophets or the evangelists. Both the misgivings of historians about the value of the ultimate ends to which they once devoted (or perhaps prostituted) their vocation, and scepticism on the part of the literate public about the capacity of historical study to effect or promote the purposes that the public currently pursues, have dethroned history from the position to which historians succeeded in exalting it in the nineteenth century. Nowadays most people seem to look to the behavioral sciences for those varieties of secular salvation which history was once supposed to provide; and some of the practitioners of those sciences seem now to be infected with the spiritual pride that once tainted the historian, pride which went and doubtless again will go before a fall.

The overall effect of the collapse of the three intellectual barriers just described has been to place historians in a more humble position in the hierarchy of general esteem, itself a salutary chastening experience, and at the same time to free them from preoccupations and servitudes unhelpful in the practice of their profession. In recent years they have enjoyed an unprecedented chance to develop their discipline free of irrelevant intellectual impediments. Although a few historians may look back with nostalgia on the time when their fraternity alone was supposed to hold all the keys to the understanding of the universe of man, the saner among them accept with relief more modest estimates of the scope and potentiality of historical studies. Men of a reasonable humility do not suffer when they are denied powers that only God could possess.

Part of the marked improvement in the quality of the best history writing in recent years has resulted from the establishment of satisfactory relations with quantification and the systematic social sciences, activities towards which the attitude of many historians had been at best ambivalent and sticky. The internecine battles among historians about these relations are just about over, and indeed it is easy for those who fought them to exaggerate their intensity. The civil wars of historians on matters of method have been rather mild affairs and have petered out rather easily in comparison with the mutual holocausts perpetrated in adjacent disciplines by the magnates and their minions.

On the point of quantification the victory has gone, as it well should have, to the quantifiers. After all, how could it have been otherwise? It is not easy even for the most zealous obscurantist to argue that historical problems which hinge on the question "how many?" are better solved by answers like "lots," or "quite a few," or "not many," or "a mere handful" than by 80, 45, 20, or 2 per cent. The statement, "The nobility, a tiny fraction of the population, held a disproportionately large share of the usable land," may strike some as more euphonious than, "The nobility, which was one-fortieth of the population, held 40 per cent of the land," but it is not likely to strike many historians as more informative. And this crude example can stand for almost all others involving quantification. In effect, in the course of their work many historians have occasion to make assertions whose validation depends on determining a particular quantitative relation—the percentage of a population, the rate of interest on mortgages, the number of voters in an election, the ratio of serfs to free peasants in a region, mean rainfall during the growing season, median age at marriage; and in such cases the sensible thing to do is to try to determine it. Senior historians naturally have not taken kindly to being challenged in some of their favorite assertions by young whippersnappers asking, "Did you count?" especially when it is all too clear that they could have and should have and did not; but only at the risk of petrifaction can a discipline accommodate its procedures to the crotchets of its obsolescent elder statesmen; and the author, well on the way to obsolescence himself, is glad that his juniors have displayed so little propensity to ancestor worship.

Increased emphasis on quantification has required historians to provide statistical foundations where they were needed. This process has been especially fruitful when it turned up evidence that the foundations were simply not there, that some long-cherished generalization about the past had suddenly achieved the poetic status of a free-floating fantasy. In one area of history after another arithmetical procedures at a level of sophistication usually attained in the fifth grade of primary school (counting, addition, subtraction, multiplication, and division of whole numbers) have provided dozens of historians with years of employment in reexploring and reinterpreting broad ranges of the "settled past" which the anomalies revealed by those procedures had unsettled. Indeed, it is possible that, historiographically, the most fruitful outcome of the increased attention to quantity has taken place at this primitive level of mathematical sophistication. This applies particularly to those periods of history in which the accumulation of contemporary statistical data, or even of data countable by a present-day investigator, is so slight or so unreliable as to blunt the cutting edge of more refined and sophisticated methods. The application of such methods to such data is like tooling, on a machine with an accuracy of 1/10000 of an inch, a ten-inch metal part with an expansion coefficient of 0.1 per cent. It is 100 times as precise as it is accurate, a waste of effort, rooted in the illusion that the ultimate sophistication can be left to the machine rather than to the person who uses it.

As the statistical data of history grow more abundant, however, the statistical methods applicable to them tend without limit towards the maximum sophistication attainable in the current state of relevant statistical methods. And that will, of course, be as sophisticated as the statistical methods used in any social science discipline, since *all* statistical data that concern or impinge upon men in their decisions, actions, and suffering are historical from the moment they are recorded and for as long as they survive; that is, as soon as they become an accessible part of the record related to something that happened in the past. It is therefore clear that for some historians of some aspects of the relatively recent past, lack of fairly intensive training in statistical methods will be a serious handicap, as serious as ignorance of archaic Greek for a close textual study of the poetry of Hesiod. But then it may be worth adding that not every philologist has to make a textual study of Hesiod.

The set of applications of statistics and the set of the application of social-science conceptions to history are intersecting; but neither wholly includes the other, and although the effective development of some recent conceptual schemes or models from the social sciences is made easier by, or absolutely requires, refined statistical techniques, other models may move along quite comfortably with only the most modest quantitative data and manipulation, or none at all. This is quite important because in the selection of their areas of investigation, historians will increasingly have to keep in mind the principle of least effort and, other things being equal, seek out those tracts where their natural or acquired skills can be applied with expectation of maximum yield.

In recent years an increasing number of historians have

shown an increasing readiness to take whatever hand up they can get from the conceptual apparatus of the social sciences, wherever they find it. They have found it in many different places. Thirty-six years ago the names of Weber, Michels, Durkheim, Freud, Schumpeter, and Keynes had no place in the lexicon, much less in the professional *Who's Who*, of historians. Nowadays they enter more and more into their staple reading, boldly acknowledged to be more worthy of the literate historian's attention than the latest monograph on Luxembourgeois Opinion on the Second Balkan War. Some historical works suggest that historians are not only taking more and more help from the social sciences, but that they are taking it more the right way. Inevitably, the vanguard who fought for an alliance of historians with the social sciences against a considerable though largely covert and *frondeur* opposition, tended to embrace their new ally passionately, indiscriminately, and somewhat promiscuously. The results were sometimes embarrassing. Too often historians discovered that the particular "latest" social-science concept they had given their love to was in fact somewhat stricken in years, had always been of suspect purity among the social scientists themselves, and now was wholly banished from respectable intellectual society. Of late, the historian oriented towards the social sciences seems to have become more discriminating, less concerned to absorb the total content of this or that social science, than eclectically to draw from any of them whatever appears to fit his present needs. Nowadays many historians casually and habitually pick up bits of the conceptual apparatus of this, that, or the other social science, try them for size on the data at hand, get what use they can out of them, and just as casually abandon them when they cease to serve their purposes. If, to social scientists, this seems a rather cavalier treatment of their brainchildren, historians may with justice reply that it is perhaps less cavalier than the use of history by many social scientists, and that anyway historians have found it helpful.

From this amiable selective plundering of the Egyptians,

there has resulted over the last few decades what can somewhat stuffily but accurately be described as an unprecedented conceptual enrichment of historiography. Fifty years ago historians had precious little to say about many kinds of historic human communities, and most of what most historians did have to say was at once jejune and naive, supported by mythopoeic notions about "natural" differences among races, people, and nations, or by a class analysis, hopelessly meager, rigid, and undifferentiated in its vocabulary of concepts, and compensatingly flaccid in its methods of applying those concepts to the record of the past. By contrast, more and more historians today display a bold, open-minded curiosity about a wide range of human communities, their ideologies and social structures, their interactions of conflict, accommodation, and symbiosis, the internal and external pressures on them, both for change and stability, and the various similarities and divergences among them. This new curiosity transforms each historian's small realm of specialization into a universe of discourse more spacious, more exciting, and more rewarding for him to inhabit and for others to explore.

Now that we have given ungrudgingly of our praise to the historians oriented to quantification and to those seeking inspiration in the adjacent social-science disciplines, acknowledging the great services they have rendered to that opening up which has so much enlivened the study of history in recent years, they may forgive us if we enter a few caveats.

Caveat I / It would be a mistake to believe that, because very important gains have been registered in historiography through the application of quantifying procedures and of concepts generated in the other social sciences, therefore all gains registered are ascribable to such application. This is not so in fact. It is not so, for example, in intellectual history, one of the currently thriving areas of historical study. With the considerable exception of a sizeable group of German historians, this field remained by and large in a deplorable condition until somewhere in the 1930s. It was under the hideous disadvantage of being at once classy, sterile, and empty-headed, suffering from a surfeit of data and a famine of thought, and paradoxically eliciting the minimal application of the historical intellect. Its characteristic product was the multivolume compendium containing exhaustive and nearly endless strings of summaries of what thinkers or pseudo-thinkers had printed in books or pamphlets on this or that topic, compendiums about as enlightening as an article in *The Reader's Digest*, if somewhat less distinguished stylistically. Intellectual history was a supreme example in historiography of the application of the Rule of the Pack Rat: (1) pick a subject about which it is certain that a lot of people have done a lot of nattering; (2) collect as much of the nattering as you can in a wholly undiscriminating way; (3) squeeze it down a bit; (4) pack it in, relying for organization on such feeble classificatory devices as date and country of issue; and (5) persuade a publisher to print as many volumes as possible. In respectable historical circles this sort of thing is no longer done, and the history of ideas now makes demands on the resources and resourcefulness of scholars which render it an unsafe and unpleasant retreat for addicts of nonthink.

In this area quantification has had only a slight impact, and the impact of the most immediately germane branch of a social science, the sociology of knowledge, has perhaps been baneful rather than helpful. It has been so because in their unseemly haste to explain why a man or a group of men thought the way they did by associating that way of thinking with a particular social context, the devotees of the sociology of knowledge have fallen into an egregious crudity of statement in setting forth what the people in question actually did think, into an egregious crudity of judgment in describing what the social situation in question actually was, and into an egregious naiveté about what constitutes a viable demonstration of causal relation between a pattern of thinking and the social milieu in which it appears. The notable improvement in the general quality of historiography in the region of the history of ideas has resulted from traits little encouraged by the sociology of knowledge: an intense concern to do the fullest justice to the integral character of what a man or a group of men intended by what they said, and a highly nuanced and tentative approach to relating thought to the society of the thinker. This delicacy of analysis and refinement of judgment, especially manifested within my range of reading in the study of Puritanism, has been achieved, to judge from the works that embody them, by historians most of whom have concerned themselves little with the social sciences. It usually results from a high level of sensitivity to rhetorical structure not conspicuously prevalent among sociologists of knowledge or other social scientists, and its most successful practitioners have often been historians whose academic training was in the literary arts rather than in the social sciences.

Another highly desirable transformation has been the emancipation of historiography from the limits imposed by nineteenth-century nationalism. It was this peculiar addiction to nationalism that, in bland defiance of the record of the past, encouraged the production of "national histories" going back for centuries and even millennia before the nations in question came into being. It also produced those strange histories running along parallel lines that met only at infinity or at the margins of what were misconstrued as international conflicts. What ultimately began the as yet incomplete emancipation of historiography from these unfortunate doings is hard to say. Perhaps a small part of it, at least, has been due to the hospitality of American universities to European history. American historians of Europe had little of the commitment of Europeans to the discovery or manufacture of a unique national identity for each European state, to be dated at the earliest conceivable chronological moment. They were therefore more ready to see what was European about Europe. Concurrently, the course of events on a larger stage has forced on the attention of historians of historiographically overdeveloped countries the potentialities for exploitation provided by many historiographically underdeveloped ones. For such historians a comparative approach, destructive of nationalist myopia, has been a common response to their task. Thus the readiness to discount national boundaries and national differences where they are irrelevant, and to be concerned with problems to which they are indeed irrelevant, seems to have grown considerably in recent years, to the profitable diminution of historical ethnocentrism. And again the contribution of statistical orientation to this emancipation appears to have been slight, and the contribution of social-science orientation, although of late considerable, not innovative.

Caveat II / The notion that in recent years all the Good Things in history come to it by way of quantification and the social sciences is not only false in fact when retrojected into the past; it is wrong in theory when projected into the future. It has not been nor is it ever likely to be true. It implies a conception of the resources available to the historical understanding far too narrow and pharisaical to do them justice. These resources are limited only by the full range of a historian's experiential knowledge, not by the exiguous bounds of his knowledge of statistical procedures and of the social sciences. In the somewhat hazy and slightly chaotic totality of an intelligent adult's experiential knowledge, such knowledge of quantification and the social sciences as he has forms precise, small, and highly organized clusters. To limit the historical understanding wholly to what historians can draw from these clusters is probably impossible. To attempt to do so is certainly foolish. Some historians in the past have done some piece of historical work so well that the chance that at any foreseeable future date any historian will imagine he can improve on it is minimal. With little or no resort either to statistics or to the systematic social sciences, historians of an earlier generation have been able to do this because they were masters of historiography, not only in their technical command of the materials they worked with but in their ability to bring a wide-ranging yet refined body of experiential knowledge to bear on a particular historical problem with extraordinary force and precision. Statistical methods and social-science concepts can effectively complement this mode of knowledge; they do not seem likely ever to become an adequate universal substitute for it.

Caveat III / Quantifying and social-science-oriented historians should not construe the awful dreariness and triviality of so much recent history writing as a consequence of the unwillingness of other historians to take marching orders from them and to follow the route they have mapped out into the historiographic Promised Land. Probably more of the dreary and trivial history recently written has been written without benefit of statistics or the social sciences than has been written with it. But that is true of the larger part of all the history recently written. Other historians will soon discover, as economic historians already have, that, like the bubonic plague of old, dullness and triviality strike impartially throughout the discipline and with approximately equal violence in all its sectors. That this should be so is not surprising. Mediocrity and futility are often not the consequence of inferior methods but of lazy and mediocre minds. While no persuasive statistical study of the distribution of such minds among the disciplines has come to my attention, practitioners of physics and mathematics say that, without an unduly arduous search, they can be found even in those rigorous studies, and that, in this respect, journals of physics reflect a state of affairs not unlike that which historians discern in their own publications. In view of the situation analyzed when we examined the first branch of our paradox—the large increase in demand and the publication rule —this was to be expected. That situation is general in the academic world, not peculiar to any of its parishes; and in the field of history as elsewhere it, rather than intrinsic methodological defects, accounts for the high triviality content of the modal product. To expect that a shift to quantification and a posture of inquiry oriented towards the social sciences will substantially raise the level of the mode suggests an optimism warranted neither by experience nor by the available evidence. The GIGO effect (Garbage In, Garbage Out) is now available by computer to some who hitherto relied on their own resources to achieve it. Although this technological improvement will almost certainly increase the GNP of GIGO, it is doubtful whether it will significantly affect its proportionate share of TSO (Total Scholarly Output).

Caveat IV / Clusters of historians fruitfully pursuing their scholarly investigations by methods that fit both the problems under scrutiny and their own aptitudes may precipitate futile and destructive wrangles, if they arrogantly press claims to the One Saving Methodological Truth. Except in lands where the sporadic testing of an orthodoxy (itself somewhat variable) imposed by the monopolists of violence is the method of achieving alternation of academic mobility and stability, there are at the moment no compelling extrinsic reasons for historians to engage in all-out *Methodenstreiten*, and up to now they have not done so. Their mutual recriminations have been tentative, their anathemas tempered, and their *autos-da-fè* nonexistent. It is well that this should remain so. This surely is the lesson of the goings-on in those adjacent disciplines, which shall be nameless, where it is not so, where the wars of method are fought to the finish. There every night becomes a night of the long knives, every day is St. Bartholomew's Day; the massacres initiated in the academic capitals spread outward and are recapitulated on a smaller scale, but sometimes with bloodier savagery, in the provinces, and the major holocausts are staged at the meetings of the professional associations where the halls and corridors are littered with slaughtered reputations of old and young alike, and made horrid by the screams of the maimed and the moribund.

It would be foolishly optimistic of historians to imagine that it cannot happen there. Recent historiography itself, and even more than that, the programmatic pronunciamentoes of various groups of historians, have shown a slightly alarming tendency to polarization; and that polarization could become painfully accentuated by men's natural propensity to claim as of right an oligopoly of scarce goods (jobs, promotions, grants, foundation and government support) for the modes of activity which they themselves find most congenial. Polarization in historiography goes on under a variety of rubrics:

> social science-oriented *versus* humanities-oriented
> quantifying *versus* nonquantifying
> analytical *versus* narrative
> *conjunctural* versus *historisant*
> "why" history *versus* "how" history
> advanced *versus* conservative

Up to now neither the left-hand items nor those on the right have been effectively forged together as weapons of internecine warfare. But a serious stroke of *Methodenstreit* would be likely to run through the *versus*, leaving some historians, like the present author, cut in two. Part of the intent of this article is to suggest an ecumenical and irenic outlook on recent achievements in historiography that would avert a civil commotion so unprofitable to the profession at large and so distasteful and discomforting to me.

Those addicted to a dialectical conception of the advancement of human understanding may be inclined to argue that the carnage of *Methodenstreit* is merely an unfortunate but inevitable and minor incident to a process that moves by its own inner laws and necessities, that the alternative lies between *Methodenstreit* and stagnation. This notion is itself question-begging, however, assuming as it does the unique merits of the dialectical model. It is, in fact, a way of thinking appropriate to a society that treats the term "revolutionary" as honorific, and indiscriminately applies it to everything from nuclear physics to razor-blade design. Whether a particular set of extensive oscillations or revolutions in the paradigms of a discipline have in fact been intellectually fruitful would seem to be a matter for empirical determination, or at least for empirical investigation. Were the matter so dealt with, one suspects it would not be hard to adduce instances where such an oscillation was ultimately propulsive, others in which its effect was regressive (going off on the wrong tack), and others in which the outcome was equivocal but costly in the economical employment of scarce intellectual energies. *Methodenstreit* would seem most likely to be regressive when, through overhasty adoption of intransigent positions, the antagonists failed to observe that the issues engaging them were spurious—essentially nonissues. This seems to be the case with respect to the tendency of some historians to divide up recent historical work into two nonoverlapping sets, each composed of intersecting subsets, and to provide for the sets normative adjectives—fruitful, scientific, precise, stimulating, seminal, gripping, imaginative; sterile, subjective, vague, trite, dull, pedestrian— distributed in a way that effectively reflects only the prejudices of the distributor.

A fully polarized general conflict of views along the lines indicated by the double list would be futile for the same reason that the specific conflicts have been futile in recent years; but by at once intensifying and confusing the nonissues it would be more troublesome and more wasteful. Recent discussions of method in history have assumed that the polarity they deal with is relevant to every existential situation historians face when they set out to write; that, regardless of the historical question that concerns him, every historian can and must opt to be quantatative or qualitative, *conjunctural* or *historisant*, analytical or narrative, and so on. This allegation is obviously contrary to the actual experience as writers and readers of history of the very people who make it; and at first one wonders how intelligent men could be so unaware of the discrepancy between what they allege all historians should do and what they actually do themselves and approve of in others. On further reflection the reason for this peculiar situation becomes evident. It is that in a period of extraordinary achievement in the writing of history, historians have neglected systematically to investigate the writing of his-

tory, and therefore their achievements and understanding in this
area have been exiguous. Indeed, the subject has been so little
alluded to that it has no name. Its former name, historiography,
has been taken over by a branch of intellectual history. Historiography has come to mean the history of the ideas of historians
about the past. Historians have neglected the investigation of
that writing of history which demands so much of their time
because of their commitment to the illusion that it does not
really count. This view has been well put and is shared by H. L.
Marrou, otherwise one of the most perceptive historians to have
written on the historian's work in recent years.

> ... An historical study will normally culminate in a written work.
> ... But such a requirement is a practical matter pertaining to the
> historian's social mission. Actually, of course, a completely elabo-
> rated history already exists in the mind of the historian before he
> has begun writing a word of it; whatever the reciprocal influences
> of these two types of activity may be, they are logically distinct
> and separate.

Consequently historians do not commit themselves to a careful
and scrupulous examination of the nature and characteristics of
good history writing. And yet quite contradictorily they treat
historiography in the sense of history writing as a unique and
significant form of human endeavor, effectively directed towards
the advancement of understanding, knowledge, and truth.

At this point in time the ambivalence and casualness of history
writers about understanding what they are doing threatens to be
too costly to continue—costly in the inefficiencies it maintains
in the education of novice historians, costly in the intellectual
waste motion involved in endlessly arguing about what writers
of history ought to do without understanding what in fact they
have done well and are doing well, and why. Even a cursory
consideration of history writing indicates that if, in Marrou's
terms, the knowledge of man's past and the writing of history
"are logically distinct and separate" (whatever "logically" means

in this context), from the point of view of the writing historian they are experientially, existentially, and operationally inseparable. The public communication of increments of historical truths so depends on the rhetoric in which they are communicated that a truth about the past cannot in fact be fully distinguished from the language in which a historian states it, and one is in grave danger of misapprehending the nature, quality, and character of the truth that history attains if one disregards historiography—the unique, significant, rhetorical form that historians are impelled or constrained to use in communicating it.[2]

One of the early fruits of an examination of historiography as it is embodied in the work of historians who write history best is highly germane to the matter of *Methodenstreit* broached above. For what such an examination shows is that very few, if any, pieces of such work conform perfectly to any, much less all, of the rubrics in the left-hand column, few, if any, to the rubrics on the right. On the contrary, most of them move back and forth across the *versus* with scant regard for the merely theoretical commitments of their own authors to writing wholly in one mode as against its converse. One may suspect that a systematic attempt to rewrite a particular piece in order to bring it into maximum conformity with any of the left-hand or the right-hand rubrics would not win the favor of its writer, no matter how firm his theoretical commitment to that particular rubric. And he would reject such a rewriting not merely because it reduced the amenity of what he had written, but because it reduced its power to do justice to what happened in the past. If these suspicions are warranted, they suggest that historians should pay more heed to what they actually do when they write history and less to the elaboration of divisive formulas not very relevant to what they do. It also suggests that the current dichotomous concepts are absurdly flat-footed and ham-handed, absurdly deficient in the precision and clarity necessary for a systematic study of history writing. Finally, it suggests that historians should think twice before they choose sides and wage a war of method over a set of dichotomies which in practice they usually treat with indifference or contempt. A *Methodenstreit* over real issues, though painful, may occasionally be unavoidable. A *Methodenstreit* over non-issues, over nothing, is pitiful. It would be rendered, one is confident, all the more pitiful by the large ability of historians to mask the absence of issues from others and themselves by the traditional opacity of their pronouncements on matters of this sort.

6 /

Garrett Mattingly,

Historian

SOME historians are by temperament or preference or natural gifts writers of articles, some of essays, some of monographs, some of full-scale comprehensive books. Garrett Mattingly was a writer of books; he wrote three of them. Of these the one known best and to the widest public is *The Armada*,[1] it is that rarity, a book by a professional historian and admired by professional historians which nevertheless became a best seller. Only slightly less well-known is his biography of Catherine of Aragon.[2] Both enjoy the current form of literary apotheosis, publication in paperback; and they will surely survive in that pantheon when thousands of volumes currently occupying a niche there have vanished. Mattingly's third book, *Renaissance Diplomacy*,[3] did not directly reach so many readers as the other two, and it probably never will; but historians of early modern Europe tend to regard it as his crowning effort. The story of a great naval battle, the biography of a Spanish-born English queen, and an account of the origin and growth of a highly specialized institution—in the hands of most professional historians these would be appropriate subjects for a typical form of academic history, the

monograph. In Mattingly's hands they became not monographs
but full-scale histories. They are so, because Mattingly had the
wide-range panoramic vision of the book writer. Whether he
wrote about the Armada, or Catherine, or Renaissance diplomacy, he saw them in their relation to the complex, richly textured
pattern of the society they belonged to. He dealt lovingly with
the detail of each of his subjects, and he was a master of the
enlivening detail. There is the young Henry VIII, with his irre-
pressible passion for adolescent pageantry, showing off his fleet,
"clad in a sailor's smock and trousers all of cloth of gold, and
blowing on a silver whistle 'so loud it was like a trumpet.' "[4] And
the peace of Good Queen Bess:

> in the midst of a Europe torn by foreign and civil war [the Eng-
> lish] remained placidly at peace. No royal taxgatherers took from
> their pockets the fruits of their industry. Prices were high, business
> good, money was plentiful; and the profits could be confidently
> plowed back into land and shipping and the growing production
> of textiles and metals in which, for the first time, England was be-
> ginning to take a notable place in the world. No soldiers clanked
> through the streets except those home from fighting in foreign
> quarrels, and a sudden knock on the door at night would be only a
> neighbor or a carter.[5]

And Henry III's preparations for the assassination of the Duc de
Guise:

> There were still some complicated arrangements to make. The
> François Ier wing of the castle, where the king slept, was a rabbit
> warren of twisty little stairways and unexpected passages. Two
> doorways, usually open, had to be blocked, and one door, always
> locked, had to be opened, so that some of the necessary actors
> could arrive on the scene unobserved. The king saw to everything
> himself.[8]

But in Mattingly's books the detail stood out from a complexly
patterned background. He did not amputate the subjects he
wrote about from the larger society to which they belonged, Latin
Christendom mainly in the age of the Renaissance. The Renaissance he defined broadly as "the critical phase of the transition

from the unified, hierarchically ordered, spiritually oriented society of Latin Christendom, to the heterogeneous, secularly oriented society of autonomous sovereign states which made up modern Europe."[7]

Although Mattingly wrote three books, his name also appears on the title page of a fourth, to which he used to refer to wryly as his *magnum opus*. In the literal sense, indeed it was, since it almost outweighed the other three taken together. The cover of that book—in the conservative drab-green buckram of the *Calendars of State Papers*, the ancient, honorable, and now archaic uniform of the Public Record Office Calendars—reminds us that the editor of the volume, Garrett Mattingly, was among other things a meticulous, precise, inordinately painstaking researcher; that he had technical equipment and proficiency unequaled by any other scholar of his generation for the kind of work he undertook; that underpropping all three books he wrote was an unsurpassed familiarity with the sources, printed and archival; that his writing only sampled and distilled, never exhausted, but sometimes almost perversely concealed his massive knowledge.

And this points to a paradox in Mattingly's historical work. The formidable patient scholar of the *Calendar* was indispensable to the witty, urbane, and brilliant author of *Catherine of Aragon* and *The Armada*, and yet the two were in a sense at war with each other. Indeed, the marks of the battle appear in both *Catherine* and the *Armada*. Both books are extremely careful and accurate and enormously erudite. But the traces of care, accuracy, and erudition are either carefully concealed or utterly obliterated. In vain will other historians seek in the place where it ought to be, at the foot of the page, for the guidance provided by that proper and useful instrument of their shared labors, the footnote. In *Catherine* the notes are somewhat shamefacedly tucked away at the end of the book, and they are so set out as to maximize the inconvenience of anyone seeking to find a particular note. In *The Armada* there are no notes at all, only sketchy bibliographical remarks on each chapter, again stacked at the end of the book, and the remarks on any given chapter are infuriatingly hard to find. Yet a reasonably full documentation, satisfying both scholarly convention and scholarly convenience, need in no way have affected the pace of either book or even involved the alteration of a word of the text. The omission was wholly gratuitous. It is as if the popular author of *Catherine* and *The Armada* were thumbing his nose at the scholarly editor of the *Further Supplement to Letters, Despatches, and State Papers, relating to the Negotiations between England and Spain, preserved in the Archives at Vienna and Elsewhere* [1513–1542], "edited by Garrett Mattingly, Ph.D." Actually the case was that of a superb and accomplished professional giving its comeuppance to a pedantic professionalism in a way which unfortunately imposed both inconvenience and sheer loss on his fellow historians.

The principal losers in the conflict, however, those that suffered from it most, were *Renaissance Diplomacy* and Garrett Mattingly himself. Mattingly suffered because he felt that somehow the best history ought to have a broad popular appeal. But the book to which he gave his most earnest thought and his most intense effort did not have it. *Renaissance Diplomacy* simply could not have such appeal; it was not that kind of book. No history of the growth of an institution in an age as remote from ours as the sixteenth century has achieved popularity within my memory; and I doubt if one ever will.

Considering that it incorporates a lifetime of the experience and the learning of a man at once erudite and wise, *Renaissance Diplomacy* is a short book. It is considerably shorter than either *The Armada or Catherine*, although its limits are wider, the problems it deals with more difficult to expound, the ideas involved more intricate. It is, indeed, too short; in a few places it is unduly elliptical, bearing the mark of an excessive compression. It should be longer; and in fact it was once a good deal longer. It ran into publishing troubles early. The American house to which Mattingly first sent the manuscript rejected it. Presumably on the grounds of its length and its limited appeal that publisher suggested he submit it to a university press, and surely at the time any of a number of university presses would have regarded it as an honor to issue the original manuscript of *Renaissance Diplomacy* with scarcely a modification. Mattingly would have none of it. To him the university press was the very symbol of that withdrawal of history into the academic citadel which he deplored and distrusted. He said that rather than turn his work over to a university press he would tear it up. Happily, he did not do that. Unhappily, he took the publisher's judgment seriously. He did not want to consign his most exacting study to the sterile wilderness haunted by the ghosts of unread historical treatises. He cut *Renaissance Diplomacy* by a third and destroyed the original draft. He never fully reconciled himself to the inevitable fact that no amount of cutting and revising could make his most remarkable intellectual achievement a popular book. It is perhaps a measure of that achievement that the *Renaissance Diplomacy* which historians read with such admiration is not as good as Mattingly could have made it; it is, indeed, not as good as he had made it. Even so, it remains one of the finest historical works of the past half century.

If any amount of skill could have made *Renaissance Diplomacy* a popular book, its author had the skill; but the cards were stacked against him. Yet as it stands *Renaissance Diplomacy* is a magnificent achievement. It scintillates with flashes of wit superbly phrased. Thus the Renaissance image of the "perfect prince" is neatly characterized and caricatured—"a shadowy figure cast by medieval idealism on the vapours of humanistic rhetoric."[8] Or, with respect to the diminishing employment of clerics as ambassadors:

Among the later writers, the instances, modern and classical, which came most readily to hand, all seemed to indicate that priests sometimes served another master than their natural sovereign. The oblique glance was, of course, at the Counter-Reformation papacy. That an ambassador who was a priest might be embarrassed by his allegiance to a Master even more exacting than the pope seems not to have occurred to anybody.[9]

In a line or two Mattingly pricks the balloon of one of the most absurdly overinflated reputations of the age—that of Louis XI. In his reign

> Guienne, ducal Burgundy, Provence, Anjou and Maine fell in, providing the main acquisitions of a king who, however much his statecraft was admired by his contemporaries, was successful chiefly by surviving his relatives.[10]

Far from being the last word in diplomatic shrewdness

> Louis was too suspicious, too devious, and too parochial to grasp all the uses of diplomacy. He could conceive of no negotiations not inspired by malice and conducted by deception.[11]

Besides the detailed and total dismemberments of conceptions—the balance of power, nationalism, the economic or rational political motivation of early modern wars—which too long have cluttered the historians' view of the age, *Renaissance Diplomacy* is full of incisive two-sentence wrap-ups of subjects on which many historians would spend pages with less to show for their verbiage. Thus, on the impact of England's defeat in the Hundred Years War:

> By the loss of its French dependencies, England had gained freedom of diplomatic maneuver. Secure behind its seas, England could now take as much or as little of any war as it liked. No commitment was more than tentative, no alliance irrevocable, and at each new shuffle in the diplomatic game the other players had to bid all over again for England's friendship or neutrality.[12]

Or on the medieval law of nations:

> In making and sustaining the law of nations, reason, revelation and custom were held to be collaborators, not competitors. Therefore the Bartolists were able to assimilate the decrees of the Church and the practices of existing governments into what they regarded as Roman Law, and, reinforcing it by the only authority left to the Roman Republic, the authority of its law schools, make *jus gentium* a living common law for Western Europe.[13]

To get so much meaning and so many ideas into so few words requires an astonishing gift for compression; but it also demands more of the reader in concentration than most amateurs of history are willing to give, and more in background knowledge than all but a very few amateurs possess. More than that, there are a half dozen chapters in *Renaissance Diplomacy* that for sheer brilliance, for depth of insight, for concise easy statement of complex and fundamental truths about the age they deal with, have few peers in historical literature. Yet only scholars immersed in the history of that age, able therefore to compare Mattingly's work with other men's, will recognize the sheer virtuosity of his performance in those chapters; the general reader is not likely even to realize that a performance to admire is in progress.

Although by all his predispositions Mattingly was a book writer, during his life he published in the learned journals a number of articles. They are not the work of a man for whom the learned article is his natural métier, as for example it is for H. J. Habakkuk. They do not—as the most successful articles do—focus on a neatly limited area and so deal with that area as to suggest or make needful the rethinking of matters of larger and more general concern. Several were *pièces d'occasion;* others were skillful, well-wrought scholarly exercises, exact (it goes without saying) in their scholarship. One of these was a virtuoso piece—a masterful and erudite investigation of the date of Shakespeare's 107th Sonnet.[14] Alone among Mattingly's writings this essay directly reflects one quirk of his career. As an undergraduate at Harvard he had concentrated in History and Literature, and for many years he taught courses in English as well as in History. The care he lavished on the seemly writing of history was the fruit of this early and long concern with literature. In a couple of other essays he made a bold foray into the region of Machiavelli studies, and from it he emerged somewhat less bashed up than most of us who have ventured onto that dark and bloody ground of learning where muddled armies clash by night.[15]

His one essay on historical writing dealt with the labors of historians on the political history of the Renaissance in the

century after Burckhardt.[16] There, Mattingly, whose public pronouncements on some of the highly touted members of his
craft were milder than his private judgments, for once let himself go in a hilarious *essai à clef*. The piece turns on the way
historians have handled three of the major political crises of
the Renaissance era—the collapse of the Italian states, the
motives of French policy from 1494 to 1559, and the causes of
the revolt and division of the Netherlands. Most of the recent
historians whom Mattingly mentions by name—Baron, Romier,
Zeller, Geyl, Valeri, Palmarocchi—come off with good marks.
The piece is an *essai à clef* because of the eminent historians of
several nations who appear anonymously as "some distinguished
names," or "deeper thinkers," or "the vanguard," or even more
facelessly as "it has been discovered," or "we hear." Anyone who
has worked in the field of Renaissance politics, however, will
recognize most of the gentlemen so discreetly disguised. Some
of them chased the hare Machiavelli started and found the
source of Italy's disaster in moral decline, papal intrigue, and
the use of mercenaries; others found the roots of French policy
in nationalism and rational political or economic objectives;
yet others asserted the inevitability of a split between the north
Netherlands and the south Netherlands as the outcome of
ancient national differences. And they were all wrong, quite
wrong. Who got the story straight? Not only the recent historians Mattingly names; but Burckhardt and, in essentials at
least, those targets-of-choice of up-to-date historians, Michelet
and Motley. Of all people! They got the essentials right, because whatever their prejudices they did not let them rule their
judgment when they sat face-to-face with the pertinent documents. If they rode their hobbies a bit, at least they did not let
their hobbies (under the alias of "new and daring interpreta-
tions") ride them.

Mattingly's earliest scholarly publication, appearing in 1932,
was "A Humanist Ambassador."[17] It cleared up a number of
details about the life of Eustache Chapuys, Charles V's resident

in England. From then on most of Mattingly's contributions to learned journals were in the nature of engineering operations on the way to or from writing books, path-clearing to ease the passage of the big battalions or tidying up after they had gone by.[18] And yet to understand what sort of historian Mattingly was and why he was among the very best of that sort, we do well to examine carefully one of his articles—"The Reputation of Dr. de Puebla," which appeared in the *English Historical Review* in 1940.[19] The article was on the way not to just one but to two of Mattingly's books. Dr. de Puebla held two firsts in Renaissance diplomacy: he was the first resident ambassador in England and the first Spanish resident outside Rome, and so he had a place in Mattingly's study of that diplomacy. He also negotiated the marriage between Henry VII's elder son and Catherine of Aragon. When the death of Prince Arthur brought that union to a premature end, he negotiated the marriage treaty which was fatefully to link Catherine and Henry VII's younger son, Prince Henry; so he had a place in the biography of that unfortunate princess. Still, these days Dr. de Puebla does not cut a very great figure in the history of his time; in the best recent survey of the Tudor period he rates one index entry and one sentence, and the judgment or valuation thus implied does not seem unreasonable.

Mattingly offered an explanation, but not a complete or wholly satisfactory explanation, for his painstaking inquiry into de Puebla's reputation. He said that he undertook it because de Puebla's "correspondence is an invaluable source for the period, [and] our judgment of his character must affect our judgment of the negotiations he conducted and our evaluation of his reports."[20] But the further one follows him into the assessment of the evidence about de Puebla, the more obvious it becomes that the initial motive ceases to be the sole and sufficient reason for the loving care, the concentrated thought that Mattingly put into his investigation. The reputation of de Puebla before Mattingly undertook to reassess it was that of an abject, pettifogging rascal, a shady trickster, scrabbling together sordid gains, and living, through avarice, in squalor; a shabby and deformed little cripple, mean, boastful, treacherous, shameless, the butt and the aversion of all he met, without anything to commend him to the rulers of Spain and England except servility, low cunning, and a complete lack of moral scruples.[21]

He emerges from Mattingly's examination the butt of a few men of his time and certainly of his aristocratic rival, Don Pedro de Ayala, boastful no doubt, devious by both necessity and temperament, cold, somewhat narrow in outlook, sensitive to slights, living meanly because his pay was too low and always heavily in arrears. He also emerges as energetic, shrewd, and patient, for over twenty years a faithful servant of the Catholic Kings, who had no appetite for being ill-served, and who requited his service with trust, but little else. He was a successful negotiator when success was possible, a resourceful one even when the course his master required him to follow doomed his efforts to failure, a man of honor, not by the standards of a sixteenth-century aristocrat but by the standards of the new profession of diplomacy of which he was a pioneer. In the end by deed or word or both, all those who knew most about him and who had no sinister interest in blackening his name—Henry VII, Ferdinand, Catherine, even Fuensalida, his successor, who ruined what little the old man wrought in the hard days of his and Henry's and Ferdinand's old age—vindicated him against all his detractors.

Vindication, of course, is the heart of the matter. Technical professional requirements may have led Mattingly to reassess de Puebla as a source of information; but somewhere along the line of inquiry the source of information became a man, the victim of an ancient and enduring wrong that needed to be set right. But why so much bother to vindicate a man really rather obscure, wholly forgotten by all but about .0000001 of men now living, dead now nearly half a millennium? To this question Mattingly had an explicit answer which brightly illuminates his own traits and his excellence as a historian. That answer does not appear in "The Reputation of Dr. de Puebla," but in *The Armada,* written two decades later. It directly has to do with another Spaniard whose qualities were better than his luck, and better than the judgment posterity long passed upon him: the grandee who commanded the disastrous enterprise against England, the Duke of Medina Sidonia.

> There is a tendency of late to speak more kindly of Medina Sidonia . . . to recognize his courage and his administrative ability, but no one has yet said he could not have done better. It is at least arguable, however, that no one could. . . . Not that such a judgment would have been much comfort to Medina Sidonia. Whatever he did, it was not enough. Nor does it matter at all to the dead whether they receive justice at the hands of succeeding generations. *But to the living, to do justice, however belatedly, should matter.* [Italics added.][22]

This casual remark, which Mattingly dropped in the course of his story, implies a whole general view of what history ought to be. Mattingly does not expound this general view in ponderous pronouncements about the nature of historical reality. As it should be with a historian, his view is immanent in the whole body of history that he wrote, and it is there that we must seek it. In the first place Mattingly believed that although history may be about any number of things—barrel staves and prevailing winds and cannons, canon law and the speed of posts and cryptography—it is also, perhaps it is mainly, about men and women and children, sometimes of necessity considered as aggregates, but often also considered as persons. But if a historian deals with men as persons, he must concern himself with human character. He must bring to play on the understanding of men of whom, in the nature of things historical, the record grants him only fragmentary glimpses, all the resources afforded him by his systematic knowledge, his experience of life, his introspection, and such wisdom as God gave him.

The historical record which is all too exiguous is also paradoxically all too full. In order to make human character stand clear of the clutter of routine action which filled the lives of Renaissance men as it fills ours, Mattingly had to practice the art of discerning and reporting the telling detail, the illuminating incident, the revelatory remark. To do this he was especially hard-pressed in *The Armada* and *Catherine of Aragon*, where the historical scene was jammed with men whose motives and natures had to be rendered intelligible quickly, lest the reader be trapped in a bewildering shuffle of wholly unmemorable names. Mattingly's judgment in such matters was immaculate. He showed it in the big set pieces—the contrasting encounters of Henry VIII with the vain Francis I and the modest Charles V;[23] Catherine's grandeur and dignity and pathos before the court that her husband had maneuvered into existence to rid himself of her;[24] Mary, Queen of Scots, magnificently playing out the last act of her life, not only before she laid her head on the block but even after the executioner had done his work.[25] But he showed it to even greater advantage in the unobtrusive detail. There is the account of de Puebla's interview with young Catherine, in which that necessarily devious old man, straightforward for once in his life, with mingled fear and anger, exposed and shattered the plot laid by Catherine's trusted duenna and her brother to undermine Ferdinand's position in Castile.[26] There is the Duke of Medina Sidonia in a short cloak, because he had given his great cloaks to a friar and a wounded boy, leaning wearily on the taffrail of his flagship as his battered fleet ran northward before the wind from the foredoomed failure of his mission in the Channel to the more terrible disaster of the long voyage home.[27] There is Philip II, who, after learning the full dimensions of that disaster, read the incorrigibly optimistic report of his ambassador in Paris, Bernardino de Mendoza, whose energy did so much to forward the great enterprise, and, having read, with his "weary pen scrawled in the margin, 'Nothing of this is true. It will be well to tell him so!' "[28]

Mattingly's way of treating human character has two notable traits. It would not be quite accurate to say that he always disliked winners—he admired Elizabeth, who almost never lost.[29] Yet he had a warm spot in his heart for those against whom the deck of life was stacked, for losers, who, having used every reputable resource at their disposal and without flinching given all they had to gain their end, met defeat as men—and women—of valor without display or self-exculpation or self-pity. Second, Mattingly does not confront his readers with a series of posed portraits interjected into a narrative at more or less random intervals. The characters he portrays are people in action. In Mattingly's books character reveals itself in what men do and say as they follow out the lines of their lives.

How was Mattingly's own work as a historian—and implicitly his view of his calling—affected by his habitual vision of the past as men acting or suffering? In practice he treated his job as that of telling a story about people. He was not dogmatic enough to say that that was what all historians ought to do, much less that it was all that historians ought to do. Yet he loved what he was doing well enough and knew that it was enough worth doing to hold in mild derision the "new wave" historians who were somewhat patronizing to him in their pride at being not narrative but analytical historians,[30] or, as some of them put it, writers of "why" history rather than "how" history. (This last widely current formulation is of such massive and stupefying naïveté that of itself it might suggest to its proponents the wisdom of deploying their powers on matters less arcane.) Indeed, in *Renaissance Diplomacy*, Mattingly himself produced the *reductio ad adsurdum* of the notion that history ought to be divided into two noncommunicating compartments, one labeled "Narrative" with "childish" painted on top, the other labeled "Analytical" with "grown-up" painted on top. For *Renaissance Diplomacy* is a masterful analysis of an institutional complex centered around a new Renaissance phenomenon—the resident ambassador. One may suppose that it answers "why" questions—whatever they are—since it answers very nearly all the serious questions that a curious mind is likely to raise about the institutions of diplomacy from the fifteenth century to the Peace of Westphalia. Yet never, one suspects, in so few pages of analytical and institutional history have so many people (not mere names) showed up, and never has so much happened. That is so because *Renaissance Diplomacy* is both narrative and analytical history.

That is as it should be. In the best writing of history, analysis and narrative do not stand over against each other in opposition and contradiction; nor do they merely supplement each other mechanically. They are organically integrated with each other; to separate them is not an act of classification but of amputation. It is an act the frequent performance of which stands a good chance of killing history altogether. Mattingly was too modest to say that whenever the historical work in progress permits, analysis and narration *ought* to be inseparably unified as they are in *Renaissance Diplomacy* and (for the benefit of the myopic, we may add) in *Catherine of Aragon* and *The Armada*; but that is of course the fact of the matter. I suspect that had he lived a few years longer Mattingly might have enjoyed the experience of others like him who dug in their heels on historical issues such as these, while their more modish colleagues marched off in the pursuit of the most recent will-o'-the-wisp. Somehow in the end the marchers come full circle, so that simply by standing still one eventually finds oneself in the vanguard.

Mattingly's uncommon concern for the losers has been ascribed to a pro-Catholic bias; and in support of such an allegation one can cite his affection for Catherine, his admiration of Medina Sidonia, his generosity extending even as far as Philip II. But against this view stands the most despicable figure in Mattingly's whole gallery, about whom "there is no mystery . . . except how so shallow an egotist attracted so many people. He was the type of the adventurer relying on a bold front and a calloused conscience, the gambler playing for stakes beyond his means."[31] Such was Henry, Duc de Guise, the idol of the French Catholics and chief of the Catholic League. Whatever biases Mattingly had were not cut along the line separating Protestant from Catholic. It just happened that the hard-pressed people living at the center of the stories Mattingly told were Catholics; had he happened to choose stories revolving around William the Silent and Henry of Navarre, no suspicion of pro-Catholic bias would have risen. It was not ideological nostalgia for a medieval dream world that moved Mattingly; it was admiration for men and women, true to themselves and their calling, responsible men and women, people of honor and courage, capable of dedication, people whose centers, as it were, lay somewhere outside themselves. Because the traits he admired are most fully tried by adversity he seemed to have a special fondness for losers. His actual predilections, however, are clearly marked in his judgment of the three great monarchs of Christendom in the earlier sixteenth century. He despised the frivolous playboy Francis I, who never grew up; he cared not much more for Henry VIII, who somehow managed the transition from reckless egocentric youth to harsh megalomaniac old age with hardly a pause for responsible adulthood. In contrast was the stolid, pedestrian Charles V. He bade farewell to youth before he was twenty; he worked with all his personal resources at the thankless, unmanageable task of husbanding the sprawling cumbersome congeries of dominions that God or chance put in his hands; and with all his congenital and political handicaps he proved a better steward of what had been entrusted to him than did either of his more brilliant rivals. Charles was a man to suit Mattingly's tastes.

Those tastes were themselves a sharp though inexplicit comment on a couple of the fashions prevailing in recent decades in the small world of professional historians. Mattingly had no use for the Big Battalion view of history in any of its manifold guises. Whether as proponents of a theory of progress, or manifest destiny, or the tide of democracy, or the self-realization of the spirit, or dialectical materialism, or the rule of the master race, historians who take the Big Battalion view of history always perceive the past in the light of their current notion of what constitutes the wave of the future. Losers are of little importance in this view of history; they are just inevitable, usually faceless, casualties of the historical steamroller, crushed because of their malice, or their stupidity, or their failure to pick the winner, or because—in one of the most callous and revolting aphorisms ever taken up by men who called themselves human- ists—"you can't make an omelet without breaking eggs." There was nothing in Mattingly's way of perceiving the past to attract him to this peculiarly vulgar form of the worship of success.

Nor could the man who wrote, "To the living, to do justice, however belatedly, should matter," ever delude himself that history could or ought to be, as some historians insist, altogether nonvaluative, wholly *wertfrei*. This does not mean that Matt- ingly, one of the least naive of all historians, believed that he should assume the posture of a Divine Sunday School Teacher handing out gold stars to the good boys of history and demerits to the naughty ones. It does mean that he knew that the vocabulary we ordinarily use in writing about men carries an ancient load of value-packed connotation. To discard that vo- cabulary is simply to discard what little capacity for judgment the cumulative experience of a great civilization has afforded us. To use that vocabulary with measure and care along with whatever means of testing the evidence and knowing the facts he can master in order to deal justly with the past is at once the historian's duty and his privilege. To do otherwise is to sur- render history's proper claim to being a practical, humane, and moral science in order to chase the foolish, fond hope of trans- forming it into a theoretical one. On this view of the matter it is no puzzle at all to know why a fine historian like Mattingly, in midcareer toward two splendid books, paused to write a long vindication of poor old obscure Dr. de Puebla. It was just the right thing for him to do.

NOTES

1 / By Way of Introduction

1. Associate membership is certified by publication of things I have written in *Encounter, The New York Review of Books, The Public Interest,* and *Commentary.* The casualness and accidental character of this associate membership is evidenced by the fact that three of the four pieces were written with no intention of trying to place them in Establishment journals and the fourth because the editor asked me to review two books that I had to read in any case. Bad standing is certified by my lack of interest in knowing about, much less reading, books that are currently "in."
2. Henrik Ibsen, *Hedda Gabler.*
3. The day after the above introduction was sent to the publisher, my colleague, Mr. Henry Avelove, pointed out to me that Michael Oakeshott had anticipated me in considering the relationship between writing history and cooking. Even more embarrassing is the fact that a good many years ago I had read the essay "Rationalism in Politics" in which Oakeshott offered his view of the relationship. There is considerable difference between us, however, since Oakeshott is struck by the contrast

between history writing and cookery, while I am struck by the similarities.

2 / The Rhetoric of History

1. Since this study was written, the "universe" of major league baseball has undergone extensive alteration. A new general law on league championships has replaced the old one in the process.
2. W. B. Gallie. *Philosophy and the Historical Understanding* (Chatto and Windus: London, 1964), pp. 22–80.
3. An approximation of this sort of thing has appeared in *The Historian's Workshop*, ed. L. P. Curtis (Knopf: New York City, 1970). The essays incline toward psycho-autobiography rather than toward macroanalysis.
4. See below, p. 172.
5. E. Harris Harbison, *The Christian Scholar in the Age of the Reformation* (Scribner: New York City, 1956), p. 93 (my italics).
6. Arthur C. Danto, *Analytical Philosophy of History* (Cambridge University Press, 1965).
7. Carl G. Hempel, "The Function of General Laws in History," *Journal of Philosophy* 39 (1943), pp. 35–48.
8. Morton G. White, *Foundations of Historical Knowledge* (Harper: New York City, 1965), pp. 220–221.

3 / The Historian and His Society: A Sociological Inquiry—Perhaps

1. *American Historical Review* 67 (1962): p. 676.
2. E. H. Carr, *What Is History?* (Knopf: New York City, 1965), pp. 24–48.
3. For a more broadly based inquiry into the function of publication, see J. H. Hexter, "Publish or Perish—A Defense," *The Public Interest* 17 (1969), pp. 60–77.
4. *Harvard Law Review* 84, pp. 485–504.
5. Ibid., p. 504. In the review the last sentence appears as a footnote to the one that precedes it above.

4 / History and the Social Sciences

1. Dating here is not intended to be precise. The writings of Buckle, Comte, and Marx bar the suggestion that I have pushed my base dates too far back.
2. For example, in the *IESS*:

GAME THEORY: I. Theoretical Aspects, II. Economic Applications. Both of these articles rely heavily on mathematical language and symbolism. The first is illustrated with a number of matrices, which have to do with matching pennies and are under various descriptions, such as a "Two person, zero sum" matrix. An example of the mathematical symbols and language follows:

Let A_1, A_2, . . . A_n be the strategies available to player A and B_1, B_2, . . . B_m be the strategies available to player B. In the resulting nxm array . . .

DECISION MAKING: I. Psychological Aspects, II. Economic Aspects. The "Index" to the most recent *IESS* has 26 listings under the "Mathematics" entry. The *ESS* has only two listings under "Mathematics" in the index. Neither of the above entries are found, the closest analogs being "Forecasting Business" by Garfield V. Cox and "Gambling" by Collis Sticking. Neither the Cox nor Sticking article relies on equations in the development of its argument and makes no reference to probability theory.

3. For example, as a consequence of the compilation and survival of the Domesday Book the number and distribution of oxen in England in the mid-eleventh century is more precisely estimatable than the number and distribution of people; and the number and distribution of all kinds of agricultural goods more precisely estimatable for England than for anywhere else in the world.

4. I owe this not precisely earth-shaking perception to two lunches and a couple of hours of talk with John McCarthy, a young colleague of mine at Yale. The aid and counsel he rendered me in the preparation of this paper adds a sixth tactical maneuver to the five discussed in this section. I call it confidential banana-peel slipping. It consists in inducing a friendly, skilled, but critical reader to go over one's work before one presents it in public. This sort of note is inadequate recompense for the enormous help that a generous colleague like Mr. McCarthy renders a fellow scholar.

5. For example, a reader of *Kommunist* could have learned of the existence of a book I wrote, *Reappraisals in History,* from a short robot-like outburst of pseudo-fury that it evoked in that journal. Whether he could actually have gotten the book and whether he would have learned anything worth knowing from reading it are questions I cannot answer.

6. This paper for example has benefitted from crisscross shoptalking with colleagues at Yale: Robert Dahl, Political Science; R. S. Hendon, South East Asian Languages; S. M. Lamb, Linguistics; J. L. McCarthy, History; E. J. O'Neill, Computer Center; G. W. Pierson, History; L. J. Pospisil, Anthropology; R. A. Roskies, Physics. Most of the men here listed came up with what I needed to know in very brief telephone conversations which they have probably forgotten about. Mr. O'Neill was kind enough to give me an hour of his time. For Mr. McCarthy, see note 4 above.

7. Theodore K. Rabb, *Enterprise and Empire: Merchant and Gentry Investment in the Expansion of England,* 1575–1630 (Harvard University Press: Cambridge, Massachusetts, 1967).

8. Rabb, p. 2.

9. Without very strong conviction I have preferred the term "order" to Rabb's term "class" here because (1) it is nearer to seventeenth-century usage, (2) it is less rigid in its specifications, and (3) it is further from the heat (without much light) of current doctrinal controversy on class in the social sciences.

10. Rabb, p. 8.

11. See his useful cautionary observations on this matter. Rabb, pp. 180–87.

12. The coding system is somewhat more refined than above indicated, but further details are dispensable here. For these details, see Rabb, pp. 141–80, 224–32.

13. Rabb, p. 69.

14. Rabb, Table 2, p. 25.

15. Rabb, Table 5, p. 66.

16. Rabb himself (p. 79) remarks on and documents from figures provided by the computer the sharp decline in number of investments, 1586–98, following hard on the failures of the preceding decade. Those were, however, good years for investing in privateering.

17. Rabb, Table 11, p. 104. I arrived at the ranking by totalling the number of gentry, knights, and peers who invested in the

enterprises. I have omitted the Irish Companies from consideration here. They were only rather equivocally overseas or maritime enterprises, and to the detriment and disaster of the Irish, one way or another, English gentry (by Rabb's definition) had been investing in "expansion" into Ireland for about four centuries.

18. This whole discussion of the amount invested in privateering is clouded by my suspicion that a great deal of it was generated by a fast plowing back of profits from one successful privateering enterprise into the next. In Rabb's discussion of sources of investment (pp. 32–34) he does not mention reinvestment. His assumption that the gentry's share in all but four of the enterprises (1.4% of the total capital in the left hand table) was "a proportion equal to their percentage of the membership" is bold indeed. For each company it involves a probable error far too large to warrant the specious precision of his computation to the third decimal place of the total share of capital.

19. Rabb, pp. 69, 101.

20. Rabb, p. 27, n. 17. Rabb does not venture a guess as to a total number of merchants in England 1575–1630, but it was surely far more than double the 3,810 merchant investors.

21. 560 out of 1,179. See table above and Rabb, p. 27.

22. Rabb, p. 32.

23. Rabb, p. 378.

24. Rabb, p. 98, n. 132.

25. Lawrence Stone, *Crisis of the Aristocracy* (Oxford, 1965), p. 564; W. G. Hoskins and H. P. R. Finberg, *Devonshire Studies* (London, 1952), pp. 336–58.

26. Any worth that the preceding critique may have derives from this methodologically naive activity. If one just wanders over the composite table above with one's eyes, it is pretty hard to miss the Big Three of the investmentscape, and it is not much easier to miss them even without the conflation. Once one has gotten some notion of the magnitude of the Big Three, other traits of imperial enterprise may assume a more coherent pattern. They may even suggest a new computer imput. What would be the consequences, for example, of refining the encoding of the gentry to allow one place for official-court gentry? Such a division coincides, after all, with a classification

currently modish among historians of the period that concerns Rabb.

27. It is at least arguable that the presence of value elements is a useful differentiating device, and that it is convenient not to regard behavior as distinctively human except when such elements are present.

28. *IESS*, Sub. Anthropology.

29. Garrett Mattingly, *The Armada* (Houghton Mifflin: Boston, 1959), p. 375.

5 / Doing History

1. This is not to deny that historical study often may have such relevance, or to asperse historians whose inclination is towards the sort of study of history that does have it.

2. From the content and tone of the previous sentences, shrewd readers may infer that at least one historian has concerned himself with historiography in the sense of the rhetoric or writing of history, that at the moment he is engaged in discreet propaganda for the importance of his own current activity, and that this propaganda is peculiarly like the kind of propaganda for their own doings which he has recently stigmatized in others. The inference would be correct; the author has already made it; and hopefully it has thereby acted as something of a warning to him. Here it may also act as a warning to others not to be conned by him into accepting his evaluations of his own activity. His preliminary efforts to look into some of the questions raised by the way historians write are contained in the first paper of this book, "The Rhetoric of History."

6 / Garrett Mattingly, Historian

1. *The Armada* (Houghton Mifflin: Boston, 1959; paperback edition, 1962), published in England as *The Defeat of the Spanish Armada*.

2. *Catherine of Aragon* (Little Brown: Boston, 1941; paperback edition, Random House Vintage: New York City, 1960).

3. *Renaissance Diplomacy* (Houghton Mifflin: Boston, 1955).

4. *Catherine of Aragon*, p. 133.

5. *The Armada*, p. 12.

6. *Ibid.*, p. 381.

7. "Some Revisions of the Political History of the Renaissance," in Tensley Hilton, ed., *The Renaissance* (University of Wisconsin Press: Madison, 1961), pp. 3–23.

8. *Renaissance Diplomacy*, p. 223.

9. *Ibid.*, p. 216.

10. *Ibid.*, p. 130.

11. *Ibid.*, p. 133.

12. *Ibid.*, p. 129.

13. *Ibid.*, p. 285.

14. "The Date of Shakespeare's Sonnet CVII," PMLA, 48 (1933), 705–21.

15. "Machiavelli's *Prince:* Political Science or Political Satire," *American Scholar*, 27 (1958), pp. 482–91; "Machiavelli," *The Horizon Book of the Renaissance* (New York, 1961), pp. 57–64.

16. "Some Revisions," pp. 3–23.

17. "A Humanist Ambassador," *Journal of Modern History*, 4 (1932), 175–85.

18. "The First Resident Embassies: Medieval Italian Origins of Modern Diplomacy," *Speculum*, 12 (1937), 423–29; "An Early Nonaggression Pact," *Journal of Modern History*, 10 (1938), 1–30; "William Allen and Catholic Propaganda in England," *Bibliothèque d'humanisme et renaissance*, 27 (1957), 333–38. Mattingly's essays on Machiavelli (see note 15 above) are in a sense of a similar character. They reveal the substance of thought behind what looks like a very casual *obiter dictum* in *Renaissance Diplomacy*, pp. 116–17.

19. "The Reputation of Dr. de Puebla," *English Historical Review*, 55(1940), 27–46.

20. *Ibid.*, p. 28.

21. *Ibid.*, p. 27.

22. *The Armada*, p. 375.

23. *Catherine of Aragon*, pp. 208–19.

24. *Ibid.*, pp. 285–87.

25. *The Armada*, pp. 2–5.

26. *Catherine of Aragon*, pp. 76–77.

27. *The Armada*, p. 340.

28. *Ibid.*, p. 363.

29. *Ibid.*, pp. 9–13.

30. Note his wickedly funny vignette of the history of history writing in America since 1900 in "Some Revisions . . . ," p. 9.

31. *The Armada*, p. 386.